"This book should be read by every parent or loved one of an autistic individual as the best model to follow for nurturing the autistic seed of genius."

)avis: Founder, The Davis Method,

Autism and the Seeds of Change

needed to regulate our own emotions, and be alert not only to what was happening with Daniel, but also what was going on within ourselves and how that might be assimilated by him." This is the art of attunement.

Parenthood is a common challenge. However, the difference between a thriving parenthood and a struggling one lies in the insightfulness of the parenting. This inspiring book highlights the very impressive insightfulness gained by Guy and Oksana during their special family journey, which is well summarised in Guy's wise sentence: *"We do not consider his autism to be an important part of who he is."*

With admiration,"

Dr. Hanna Alonim,
Director, The Mifne Center

Transforming Autism:

How One Boy's Life Was Renewed

by Guy Shahar

For more about *The Transforming Autism Project*,
visit us at: http://transformingautism.co.uk/

Guy Shahar's collection of stories, *Leaving Town*,
is available in paperback and Kindle versions from
Amazon in most countries, including amazon.com.

Contents

Introduction

I am not an expert on autism. Far from it. I would be hard pressed to give more than a basic description of what it actually is. But I have lived through my son, Daniel's, first six and a half years as an autistic boy, using my limited research skills to find ideas, therapies and attitudes that would improve his quality of his life, and using my heart and intuition (along with my wife's) to follow up on them. In that time, he has gone from being a lovely joyful baby, to a 2 year old who was almost totally cut off from the world around him - including his parents - and heading for a life of serious disability, to a happy 6-year old attending a mainstream school with an unspeakably beautiful character. There is still some way to go, particularly around his awareness and understanding of social interaction, but he is going there and we are going there with him, and we are confident that we will get to where he needs to be.

In the 5 years since Daniel's symptoms first became

apparent, especially for the first half of that period, looking after him, facilitating his development and finding therapies that would support his evolution has been our driving force, and we have cultivated certain attitudes to help us in this. Most importantly, we feel, is trusting our instincts; not in a rash way and not dismissive of anything new that didn't instantly appeal, but equally not wasting time and energy on paths that were clearly not going to get us anywhere (and which were probably going to drain us dry) just because they were what most people were expecting us to follow. Instead we explored with relish options that we did have a gut feeling might help us, even if we didn't fully appreciate how, and even if some of them might at first glance have appeared a bit oddball. We have thus been on a journey where we have wasted a lot of money on useless things that have made no difference, but have also discovered some really remarkable approaches, including two in particular which have been very significant in his recovery, and which I will describe at length. Through them, we have learnt that "treatment" cannot be divorced from daily life and the environment we create around our son, which is the backdrop to his entire experience of the world and the most critical factor in his well-being and progress.

My wife and I have been extremely lucky to have been on the same page about most of it and we have learnt that it is critically important for parents to have a similar understanding of what approaches they feel are right for their child - and at least to carry a consistent and genuine respect for each other's inclinations when there are differences We also recognise that we have been unusually fortunate in the leads that have been placed before us and the amazing support we have had in implementing them, and it is this good fortune that has made all the difference. It has turned our son's life, and our family's life, around and enabled us to appreciate the silent richness that was always there inside Daniel. When I see other children who are severely autistic and clearly suffering from a high degree of frustration, I feel tearful and want to reach out to them, knowing that hidden within each of them is a deeply sensitive and perceptive human being, full of pure intentions, trust and goodwill, who longs to share his good-nature with the world, but is simply overwhelmed and subject to continuous profound shock from the sensory stimulus all around and from the animated, emotional displays, sometimes less than friendly, that other humans consistently exhibit both towards each other and sometimes to them.   In reality it is not possible to walk up to them and expect to be able to just reach them and make a difference to their lives right there and then, and it is so deeply frustrating not to be able to share what we have learnt and all the possibilities that have been made available to us with them and with their parents or carers - not to mention with all the families I will never meet. This book is my attempt to share some of what our family has been so fortunate to receive, in the hope that it will resonate with at least someone and play its part in the transformation of their family's life. Much of what has been revealed to us, we have not found clearly described anywhere else.

I will discuss the various paths we have taken, but with an emphasis on the attitudes we have cultivated and the environment we have learnt to create around Daniel in his daily life, as these have made by far the most difference. In fact, what I hope to do in this book is to transform the way that we see autism and our relationship with autistic children away from looking at it as a problem that some children have that needs to be treated in the hope of curing it or lessening the symptoms. Instead, I propose that we try to understand the inherent characteristics of our autistic children, recognise the nature of their tremendous strengths and do what we can to bring out the best in them.

When discussing therapies that we have tried, I will be open about what has and hasn't worked for us. However, it is never my intention to promote or dismiss any particular therapy. It is often the case that the success of any therapy depends at least as much on the calibre of the therapist as on their method. For example, I believe that homeopathy potentially has much to offer, but *our* experience of it has not been very inspiring, with one friendly homeopath offering as the major contribution for his £65 fee, "I think I would give him 1000mg of vitamin C daily to help with his immunity". It is not easy to find an effective practitioner when there are so many out there and the really effective ones are so few. A personal recommendation is probably the only way, or failing that, an appeal for one on the various parenting forums. But there is no getting away from the other part of the issue, which is that what works for one child might not work for another. Every child is different, and the silent torments that each autistic child craves release from are not the same. So please take my observations as personal ones that apply to our family, based on our own experiences and which may be of use as a general guide to others. And I would like to emphasise again that it has not been any therapies that have made the most difference to us - it has been the surrounding conditions that we have learnt to bring into our life and Daniel's - and the "therapies" that have truly helped have been those that have focussed us on the more universal question of how we do this. In this way, they have taught us to be better parents than we could ever have hoped to be by ourselves, autism or no autism. These are the principal things I wish to share in this book.

My profound best wishes to all who are embarked on this involuntary but potentially highly fulfilling journey.

Chapter 1 - The Beginning

In the opening minutes of Sunday 16th August, 2009, my wife, Oksana, was struggling after an exhausting 13 hours of labour. Her waters had broken (3 weeks early) on the Thursday, but the contractions hadn't become strong enough, so on the Saturday morning, she was induced. Shortly after midnight, the midwives decided to get the forceps, but before they had a chance to use them, Daniel suddenly burst out in a state of evident bewilderment. As Oksana had torn severely, I had him for the first 20 minutes or so of his life, while she was stitched back up. He didn't cry or seem distressed, he just stared around the room with wide eyes. He was very small - well under 3kg - and a little jaundiced.

Daniel's first utterance was when one of the midwives whisked him off me, washed him, and counted out each of his fingers and toes slowly and with what I felt was unnecessary firmness. He wailed, and I understood his wailing. As he wailed, she laughed and joked loudly,

"Oh, they don't like this part!"

During his first days in the hospital, where he and Oksana needed to stay while she recovered from the labour and the subsequent blood transfusion, he seemed quite settled, though unusually sensitive to bright lights or sudden loud noises, of which there were plenty. But when we got him home, he seemed perfectly fine. He slept peacefully in his basket, easily took to the breast and generally seemed contented.

This changed several days later. The health visitor came round to take a sample of blood from his foot (or perhaps it was to give him a vitamin K injection). In order to minimise the distress this might cause him, Oksana put him on the breast. He didn't stop feeding, but let out a muffled groan as they pricked him. It looked like a brief moment of relatively minor distress, which had passed and was now over. But from that evening, everything was different. There were no more peaceful uninterrupted sleeps. He began to toss and turn uncomfortably as soon as he started to sleep and right through until he woke. As he grew, he needed increasing amounts of motion in order to be able to start to sleep at all. He was no longer able to sleep on his back as he had in the early days, instead continuously shifting uncomfortably to try to find an acceptable position, always turning awkwardly to the right. He started to wake up screaming quite often, and would only sleep on top of his mother. They had many uncomfortable nights of very disturbed sleep together, with Daniel lying on Oksana and waking unhappily several times each hour. Even more alarming was that he soon started intermittently to forget how to feed from the breast. He would begin feeding, and then, having let the breast fall out of his mouth, he seemed unable to be able to take it again, which caused him much distress. Sometimes, this went on for long periods (strangely, finishing more often than not at 12.15am, the time of his birth). We didn't want to take the breast away from him, as this might distress him even more, and we didn't want to introduce formula milk too early for fear that he would give up on the breast and all its benefits, especially as he still seemed to be getting milk from it. But as it became clear that this was not just a phase, we did turn to formula and to expressing milk.

Even though these issues clearly began with the blood sample, it would be too easy and simplistic to deduce that it "caused" developmental issues. Even if it was the trigger, what was it about Daniel that pre-disposed him to such a reaction to it, when most children had none?

About 3 weeks after Daniel's birth, there was a reunion of our anti-natal class, as all of the babies had been born by then. Although Daniel was by no means the last to be born, we noticed how immature he looked compared to the rest of them. He was not quite the smallest, but he seemed almost embryonic in the alertness in his eyes to his surroundings, and even his awareness of his own body.

So there were some very clear early signs that something was not as it "should" be, but we didn't yet suspect anything more than a difficult start. Parenting was supposed to be a challenge, after all. After a few weeks, Daniel's feeding issues started to subside and he was gaining weight, supplemented with increasing amounts of formula milk. His sleep was still disturbed - he didn't get enough and was constantly waking up, and even seemed to resist our attempts to help him to sleep. But with the improvement in his feeding and the absence of any new issues, if we had had any concerns, they would have been fast receding. There was enough "not right" for other people to occasionally tentatively ask questions about whether he was okay, but we didn't recognise that there was anything in such questions.

Developmentally, the expected milestones were reached - often a little on the late side, but nothing to be worried about, especially as he had been born slightly premature. By 4 months, he was smiling and gurgling at us, and by 6 he was laughing a lot - both at hilarious things, like a spoon being tapped on the side of a glass (fortunately, he has retained his quirky sense of humour), and at sudden noises and faces that we made for him. He was making direct eye contact with us and interacting with us while laughing.   There was a period at around 7 months when he was crying inconsolably for no apparent reason (nothing to do with teething at that time), but this passed.   He started eating puréed food, and by 9 months was very attached to us, wanting to be held by us much of the time.   Soon after this he was crawling and exploring places and being fascinated by new things he found and he generally seemed like a very content baby.   He also had a warm and outgoing personality and loved to be around other people. He didn't directly play with other children, but was very happy to be near to them, and when in public places, often made lovely eye-contact with other adults, or walked up and touched them playfully.   He was open and full of joy.

Around this time, he became increasingly attached to me, which lasted for nearly a year.   If I put him down or passed him to someone else, or went away somewhere, he would cry for me and want to come back to me.   This was very nice for me, but could be quite extreme at times, and was one of the first signs of some sort of emotional imbalance, though, understandably, I wasn't keen to recognise it as such.

When he started exploring things and places that (according to us) he shouldn't be, we gave him a firm "no!", and his reaction was to burst into tears.   This is not unusual in itself, but these were clearly not tears of protest or of frustration; they conveyed a surprising sense of hurt in them, perhaps that someone he trusted so implicitly had treated him with such 'violence'. At some level, we must have registered that at the time, and we quickly stopped expressing ourselves in that way.

By 1 year, he was walking and pointing, and soon after that began to make word-like sounds for "Mama", "Daddy", "No", etc. and started to eat solid food. This led to the next thing that started to worry us, and much more so: a couple of months after beginning on solids, he started increasingly to allow some of the food to fall out of his mouth while he was chewing it, even his favourite snacks like crisps and biscuits. It was as if he had forgotten how to swallow. Soon after that, my wife reported that he often seemed cut off, staring into space without any apparent interest in anything. I hadn't noticed it, and we later worked out that this was because he was more engaged when in my presence due to his continuing attachment to me, although eventually, that went too.

While he had always loved animals and behaved gently and protectively towards them, he now began to chase birds in the park and deliberately stomp past the geese resting by the side of the lake, forcing than to jump into the water and uttering a flat, "bye bye" at them. We were sad to observe this, but put it down to a normal phase of boyhood, however much it contrasted with his earlier character, noting that some children were at least as uncharitable.

After around 18 month, full regression slowly started to become evident and we could no longer look at each of his unexpected behaviours as isolated issues; there was clearly something more serious and fundamental going on. He became devoid of energy and more cut off, even from me, spending more and more of his time either blankly staring into deep space, or lying on the floor rolling a toy car backwards and forwards. When he did "play", it had to be alone, and much of it was doing the classic lining up his cars or other toys in neat lines, and being very protective of keeping them there. If we ever tried to join in, for example when he was looking through the pages of a book, he completely ignored us. If we tried to point to one of the pictures, he would casually take our hand and move it to the side like a disembodied annoyance, without even looking at it. He also began determinedly ignoring other children when in their presence. He started to salivate and dribble more from the mouth and developed involuntary arm movements and flapping. We noticed less and less eye contact from him and an increasing resentment of any form of communication, showing particular displeasure at being addressed by name, however softly. He gradually lost the words he had learnt, and within a few months had lost the ability even to formulate hard consonant sounds, communicating - on those few occasions when he felt inclined to communicate at all - using only slurred grunts and droning sounds. Sometimes, he would spontaneously laugh for no apparent reason or rock with excitement. He started demanding more and more impossible things of his toys, like balancing them in ridiculous ways or trying to force big things into little spaces, and getting very distressed when he couldn't do it - occasionally resorting to self-harm as an outlet for his frustration. I was particularly shocked one day to find him in a state of anger with his toys banging his teeth against the table, albeit guardedly, seemingly in a deliberate attempt to inflict pain on himself. He started to behave differently around food - taking fork-fulls from his plate and rather than eating them, shaking them back onto the plate or the floor, apparently having lost the understanding of what they were actually for. He gradually lost the ability to swallow solid food at all, and refused most of the time to take even puréed food from us. The only way we could get him to eat anything was to put on a cartoon so that his attention was absorbed, and spoon feed him specially puréed meals. Even then it took up to an hour, or sometimes more, to get a small bowl of food into him. We took this opportunity to at least make his diet as ideal as we could - we made sure that he was consuming large amounts of fresh organic fruits and vegetables, pulses and whole grains, ground seeds, and so on, and adding critical supplements to his meals like Cod Liver Oil, Vitamins D and B12, none of which are the typical fare of 18 month old children (and which, to be fair, made the food taste pretty disgusting).

He developed strong and inflexible dependencies and aversions. For example, he became deeply stressed and panicked when approaching a door that he wasn't familiar with, and refused to go through it. He became more and more attached to his pushchair, eventually refusing to go anywhere without it, and wailing incessantly if it went in a direction that he didn't want. He started to insist on sleeping in it during the daytime (for increasingly long sleeps) with the plastic rain-cover over it, and refusing to leave it on waking, screaming in intense protest if the plastic cover was even lifted. He hated being undressed in any way, even in the boiling heat. One day, when it had been quite cold in the morning and we had dressed him warmly, we were pushing him through Hyde Park when the temperature reached well over 30 degrees, yet still he adamantly refused to have any layer of his clothing removed, even though he must have been baking hot in there.

And then there were the meltdowns - sometimes with no apparent cause, sometimes seemingly due to his toys not conforming to whatever new unscientific law he had tried to dictate to them. It was as if his distress about such things stayed with him and accumulated over time -

with new instances of stress adding to it - until he became unable to contain himself any longer and it all spilled out in epic proportions.   He became utterly inconsolable for long periods, screaming in what looked and felt like utter devastation, and finally, when exhausted, sobbing himself breathlessly to sleep.   We felt to take fewer and fewer pictures and videos of him during this period - it just felt wrong to record this, and was not the sort of memory we wanted to preserve for posterity - but we did take a few to give to those who would treat him so that they could have an understanding of what was going on at home.   There is one particularly distressing video of my mother trying in vain to lovingly comfort and calm him with any means she could find, but being unable to make any difference to his profoundly distressed condition.   It is sobering now to think that we lived through such situations and that Daniel actually experienced that degree of distress, sometimes several times a day.

There were a few signs of hope, and indications that something of the boy we had known remained alive. There were some rare moments of interactive play amidst all of this.   He would occasionally react to being physically chased.   He wouldn't look at us, but would run away excitedly and with a light laugh.   He might once in a while join in a simple dancing game for a moment.   He would still react to peek-a-boo games, occasionally even with eye-contact.   He went through a short phase of grabbing any nearby adult, making them sit on the sofa and then spinning round in front of them, clearly enjoying the attention and applause he got. Physical contact never totally died out, though his engagement in it became passive. He didn't completely give up on the breast until he was 22 months, and he still had warm reactions to certain things, for example when he came across a cat or a dog. And he never became violent towards us, apparently careful even in states of deep frustration to avoid causing harm to other people. Even by early summer 2011, as he was approaching his second birthday and things were looking increasingly bleak, there were occasional instances of interaction. By that time, there was no eye-contact at all, except when he was lost in cartoons, which seemed to be the only time he would come alive and get excited about anything. When he saw something especially funny or a sound that he liked while watching them, he would look at us as if to somehow want to share the experience with someone. Looking back, we are sure now that this is what he was wanting to do, because it the same look he gives us now when wanting to share something he is enjoying. There was also one time when I was out walking with him, and while carrying him home, I felt in an unusually light and positive mood and bounced him up and down much more than usual. There was little indication of any response; he continued staring out to the side and into space with the same (lack of) expression on his face. I wasn't sure, but I felt there was an almost imperceptible curving upwards of the corner of his mouth into what would have become the beginnings of a smile if it had gone any further. This made me extremely happy and in some way connected with him. I felt silly making such a big deal of something so tiny and probably in my imagination anyway, but it did somehow feel very significant. During Daniel's later improvements, we became familiar with this very subtle facial expression as he started to learn to enjoy things again, and it is clear now that this was a rare instance of his feeling happy and in some way engaged with us at a time when all engagement seemed to have totally disappeared. I wonder how many more instances there were and how many more signals he was giving us that we could have built on if we had understood or even noticed them.

That question would return in the autumn, but at this time, we felt totally useless and ill-equipped to know how to build even on those few signs of hope that we were able to perceive. We knew that there must be *something* we could do to connect with our boy - to invite him back into our lives and to make him feel happy there - but we had no idea what it was. Instead we felt like impotent witnesses of a tragic estrangement between ourselves and Daniel, and looked around desperately for any sort of therapy that would help him. We cried together practically every day during this most difficult period.

It is interesting to remember that even through these darkest times, we never thought of Daniel as being seriously autistic. We assumed, despite the obvious severity of his symptoms, that if he had a condition at all and that if it was autism, it was probably a fairly mild case. We pressed for it to be investigated, but never had any inkling that it could have been as profound as it actually was. It is only in retrospect that we can see what a situation we faced, and it seems now that it could have been so easy for us as parents to delude ourselves into thinking that even if everything was clearly not fine, it was not as serious a situation as many other people have. Fortunately, we were driven to get the best outcome for Daniel whatever the level of his disability.

When Daniel was born, we had bought only one book on parenting, by Margot Sutherland, and had never read it. By the time he was 20 months old, both ourselves and my parents simultaneously had strong suspicions that what he had was autism, and as a first point of investigation, we took this book and looked under "autism" in the index to find one solitary reference. We looked it up, and there were barely a few lines. They made passing mention of a clinic called the Mifne Centre in a village in the north of Israel, which, it said, was having exceptional results in reversing the emerging symptoms of autism in babies and toddlers. We researched it, contacted them, connected on Facebook with a family that had previously been there, and we both felt extremely positive about the place - not only because of the results that they were having, but also because of the approach that they seemed to take, which was purely about connecting warmly with the child and gradually, through a very human down-to-earth method of child psychotherapy, encouraging and nurturing the inherent trust and will to communicate and to be a part of a loving community that is inherent in every person, but usually deeply hidden in autistic people. It felt like a very real cause for hope. The only problem was that it was extremely expensive and there was no way we could afford it[1]. On the other hand, we had a child with increasingly severe autism that nothing else was making any significant difference to, and we both had a strong feeling, which felt much more profound than a desperate hope, that this could genuinely change our family's life. We took the rash decision to go there, and to worry about the expense later.

It was the best decision we have made during the whole of this Daniel's life (and we were only able to make it due to very generous contributions from both our parents). I will write about our experiences there at length in Chapter 3. But before we got there, we had to endure an excruciating and profoundly demoralising and

[1] I should note that the expense was due to the involvement of many people over an very intensive 3-week period, and that the Mifne Centre is a non-profit organisation. In the event, they were actually able to obtain funding to subsidise a third of the cost of our treatment due to the financial difficulties that we would otherwise have encountered.

exhausting summer negotiating the UK medical system.

Chapter 2 – Dealing with Doctors

It is natural in times of any sort of major health difficulty to turn to medical professionals for guidance and treatment. This is what we did, as soon as we became concerned with Daniel's developmental regression. The experiences we had in our initial months of doing so were very fortunate in only one sense: in the sense that they forced us to understand very early on that if we were going to be able to make any appreciable difference to Daniel's life, we would need to step outside the mainstream medical system and take full independent responsibility for his development ourselves. Their support was at its best non-existent or well-meaning but too generic to be of any use; and at its worst, confrontational and utterly compounding of the difficulties that Daniel was facing. In all cases it removed any grounds for hope.

It started with some initial visits to Daniel's friendly

GP in early 2011 when he was approaching 18 months old, and we could no longer ignore what was happening to him. She listened sympathetically and explained reassuringly that this was probably just an unusual blip in his development - certainly nothing to be too worried about at this stage - and that there was no need to refer him to anybody. We should just keep an eye on him and come back if nothing changed.

So we did keep an eye on him and nothing did change, except for the worse, so we went back. Again, she said that referring someone so young to a paediatrician was not usual for symptoms like these and she was reluctant to do so. She told us again that we should just keep an eye on him and if we were still concerned after a few weeks, then she would put us on the waiting list to see a paediatrician for advice. She did, however, refer him for sight and hearing tests, to rule out poor vision being a cause of his not making eye contact with us, and poor hearing being a cause of not responding to his name. This seemed surreal to us, and we told her that we could easily observe that both his sight and hearing were very acute, but she told us that this was the process and they had to rule these things out before taking it any further. We obediently took Daniel for these tests, and of course both his vision and his hearing came out as very strong.

Things only deteriorated, so after about a month, we

returned to get our referral to a paediatrician. I took along a comprehensive but concise report in the form of bullet points which gave a close to complete picture of Daniel's situation that was quick and easy to read and assimilate. I did this for all appointments with anybody from then on, as it enabled that information to be imparted in a few minutes at the start of the session and allowed time to follow up on the parts they needed to know more about, rather than spending most of the session talking it through from scratch and leaving no time for anything else except booking a follow up appointment to do the same a few weeks or months later. Wherever I could, I sent this in advance, so they even had a chance to read it before we arrived.

However, the GP was by that time away on maternity leave, and her replacement was much more hard-line. My report painted a bleak picture of where we were, but she dismissed this as part of the normal fluctuations of child development, suggesting that the problem was probably that we just didn't know how to discipline our child properly and saying that no child would be referred for any further investigation for such symptoms until they were at the very least 3 years old. That was a year and a half away, and we couldn't imaging getting no support for so long. Nothing could change her mind on this. Reasoning didn't work, pleading didn't work, citing the previous GP's assurance that we could have a referral didn't work, even asking whether she would accept such a decision if this happened to one of her own children didn't work (she said she had full trust in the system) and we went away with nothing except frustration and despair.

The next time we went, I think it was 2 or 3 weeks later, we were more insistent on our rights, and she was more yielding. She put us on a waiting list to see a Clinical Paediatrician. There would be a long wait - up to 3 months, which seemed like a long time to manage the situation - but at last we were going to get guidance and support from an expert who would know how to help our son regain his vitality and balance.

Eventually, after more degeneration in Daniel, our appointment came through for 28th June 2011. Daniel was at his worst point during this period, and we were in desperate need of help. We took him hopefully to the hospital and were greeted by a friendly consultant who congratulated me on my clear report, which I had sent in advance and which she said was very useful (indeed, the bulk of her own report that she later sent back to the GP was taken directly from mine rather than from any observations of her own). She said that she wanted to wake Daniel, who was sleeping in his pushchair there, undress him and give him a full and thorough examination. We reminded her that one of the things we had written in the report was Daniel's by that time very pronounced aversions both to being woken and to being undressed, and expressed our concern about how much it might distress him to be woken up *and* undressed in a strange place by someone he had never seen before. She explained patiently, but with a hint of weariness, that she understood this concern and that we needed to trust her. She was a professional who had worked with children with all sorts of disabilities for 25 years. She knew how to handle sensitive children and conduct examinations effectively with the minimum of distress. Reluctantly and with some anxiety, we gave her the go ahead. She woke him gently, and he started to scream as usual, which seemed to surprise her a little. She explained to him gently that she needed to take off his shirt to look at him and help him, and carefully started to undo the buttons. Daniel went into a complete meltdown and she suddenly looked startled and lost. She was clearly unable to go any further. Oksana took him outside away from her, and he remained in a state of hysterical, terrified screaming in the corridor for 40 minutes. Later, in the evening, he suffered his most severe meltdown to date, screaming and writhing like an animal in agony for almost an hour. The only mention of this incident that she gave in her report to the GP the next day was "I was unable to examine his ears or his eyes as he was very uncooperative".

So the hope with which we had gone to see this consultant was totally shattered. We had waited for weeks for this appointment, expecting some sort of meaningful guidance or treatment or advice that would make at least some small difference to our lives, and all she had done was to prod Daniel's sufferings with a hot poker. We walked away with nothing except a couple more referrals to go onto a couple more waiting lists for a few more weeks; one to see speech and language therapist for another hearing test(!), one to see a community paediatrician "to assess the possibility of his having autistic spectrum disorder", and because our report had mentioned some bangs he had had to the head at various times, we got a referral for an MRI scan as well. That was it. It was all about either ruling out what were really quite unlikely causes, or in the case of the autism investigation, assessing his symptoms with a view to categorising and diagnosing what name they would give to them. But nothing that would be of any use in improving the quality of his life. It was staggering to us not only that someone with so much specialist experience and with such self-proclaimed confidence could have proved so inept, but also that in spite of the very clear needs that we had for help, support, guidance or anything that would make Daniel's life and our lives better, nothing at all was forthcoming. It was a massive further blow to our trust in the system. But it wasn't the last one.

The last one began the following day. While still recovering from the stress of that hospital visit, we received an urgent phone call late afternoon from the children's ward of the hospital requesting us to bring Daniel back in that evening for a CT scan to be conducted under general anaesthetic overnight. They explained that in view of the urgency of this situation, they didn't want to wait until the MRI machine was next available to check for a fracture to his skull, so were going to make do with a CT scan for now, and to do it as soon as possible. This was a big surprise to us . We were used to waiting at least weeks for anything to move, not for the doctors to be taking the initiative, and so pro-actively. We asked why it was so urgent, and although they didn't have any sort of coherent reason, the seriousness of their tone persisted. Naturally, we weren't keen to introduce a new panic in to Daniel's life or our own if it was not absolutely necessary, and general anaesthetic for a CT scan sounded a bit extreme, so we asked whether it could be done on another day. As an unhappy "compromise", they grudgingly offered us the option to come in as day patients the following morning for Daniel to be scanned under sedative.

When we arrived, we were greeted by another very polite and friendly consultant, who listened sympathetically to what had happened 2 days earlier with the paediatrician, and to our strongest wish to avoid anything like that ever happening again. She said she understood and that they would make this day as comfortable as possible for Daniel. He would be able to go to sleep naturally and the sedative could be administered orally by syringe as he slept, so there would be no need for any disturbance to him. She explained the extreme urgency as being related to a perceived risk of a brain tumour that would need to be detected and treated immediately, though this didn't seem very probable to either of us. Then, however, while retaining her politeness, she started to bring in a warning tone, telling us that there were enough people worried about Daniel that the Child Protection Act would be invoked if we refused to cooperate with the scan, as we had refused to come in the night before (we hadn't refused, we had simply expressed out reservations and asked to arrange a mutually convenient time).

Putting this to one side (it was too much to take on at that moment), we took Daniel for a walk to help him sleep, and when, after a long time, he eventually did, we returned to the ward for him to have his sedative and his scan. But there was a complication. The staff had failed to go through the normal admittance process with us, meaning that he had not been weighed on his way in. Without knowing his exact weight, they didn't know what dose of sedative to give him, and so could not proceed. The consultant informed us of this as a simple matter of fact, saying that Daniel would have to be woken and given the sedative. I reminded her that we had spoken about how we didn't want a repetition of what had happened with the paediatrician 2 days earlier and asked whether his scan couldn't be postponed until he woke up naturally. She suddenly became very impatient, accusing us of "obstructing" their attempts to scan him after they had had to chase us 4 times(!) to even get us there. She told us that while we might have spoken about what had happened a couple of days earlier, we had not explicitly made the request, "I do not want you to wake him," and therefore she did not feel bound by it. And anyway, all the appointments are carefully scheduled and changing his time would cause disruption to all the other patients in the whole region. When I tried to answer each of these points in turn, she became more intense, interrupting and saying that she had lots of other patients to attend to and didn't have time to spend any longer with us. So I told her that we would not refuse the scan, but we would refuse them doing it in this way, and that if they wanted to wake him, she would need to invoke the Child Protection Act as she had threatened, and we would fight her all the way, and if we didn't succeed, we would determinedly seek redress later. She became more thoughtful and replied more quietly, "I know" and ended the conversation. Shortly after this, they agreed to wait until he woke by himself.

At the time, although stressful in the extreme, this all seemed more bizzare than anything else. The talk of our obstructing their tests and of using the law to bypass us seemed to make no sense whatsoever. It was we who had been seeking intervention in the first place and all we had ever objected to was their incompetence in delivering it. But looking back, putting the pieces together in our mind - what they were saying and how they were speaking to us and looking at us - it is now clear that they believed that we had, either deliberately or through negligence, inflicted a series of head injuries on Daniel, and they were looking the evidence to prove it, with a view to either charging us with abuse or removing him from our care. If they had done that, the consequences would have been unthinkable. I don't think he could ever have recovered from the scar of being removed from his loving parents, especially at such a time of difficulty for him, into the hands of people who had shown themselves to value process (at which they were anyway very poorly skilled) far above the human needs of a suffering child. It is very fortunate that we did not tune into this undercurrent of the situation at the time, as I genuinely have no idea how we would have reacted. I don't imagine the outcome would have been very productive.

Of course, there was no fracture, no haemorrhage, no tumour, and when we did go down for his scan, there was nobody either before or after him, and so, happily, any disruption we caused to the whole region's appointment schedule appeared to be minimal. We had been led to believe, and had very much hoped, that we would have completed the scan by lunchtime and would be able to take him home to rest in the afternoon after a traumatic week, but it was late at night by the time we got out of there. The sedatives didn't knock him out, so they just gave him more. They ended up giving him 3 types (for the record, they were Chloral Hydrate, Midazolam and Alimemazine), and it took him hours to go to sleep. It would have been better to have waited until he was naturally ready for his next sleep. The drugs just made him weak and seemed to restrict his ability to move his limbs. It was heartbreaking to see our already challenged boy trying for an extended period to drowsily crawl around on the bed he was on but lacking the strength to do so.

Looking back, I can't help feeling that they were disappointed to be letting us go; not having found a fracture, but still convinced, for some reason, that they were sending Daniel back into a life of abuse. They made other appointments for us, for an MRI scan and a skeletal scan, but we slowly rescheduled them and postponed them and eventually wriggled out of them altogether.

And that was it. That was our relationship with the regular medical system at an end, and we weren't parting on good terms. We felt utterly violated, disrespected, not treated like humans and completely let down. And absolutely wiped out emotionally and physically. I had been on a few days of compassionate leave from work to sort out all of these things, and I remember the morning following this visit, lying exhausted on the floor in an upstairs room, barely able to move, speaking to my manager on the phone, who listened disinterestedly to a brief summary of what had happened and then asked me bluntly when I would be back at work, as he needed his full team there. Not only did he need me back, but he needed me to be fighting fit and fully focussed on the job without any distractions. I don't think I have ever felt so overwhelmed by my life situation as I did on that day.

Something had to change. All we were getting from the medical establishment were dashed hopes and deeper problems. Even if we continued relying on them, what would we get out of it? We started to observe other families' experiences with them; the amount of effort they were required to put in to get the tiniest results. The steps to an autism diagnosis seemed to involve constantly chasing professionals all the way, trying desperately to convince them to believe what they were being told about the children in their care, to take any action, or to make any recommendations or referrals. And if they ever succeeded, all that seemed to come out of any consultation was a report or assessment, based largely on what the consultant was told by the parents along with some simple superficial observations made during the few minutes spent together. Occasionally, they might be accompanied by some generic suggestions that may or may not be moderately useful in managing some of the symptoms the child displayed. The autism diagnosis itself just seems to be a sort of mega-assessment that provides a label for the child. Very little of any use follows from it, apart from the occasional under-resourced batch of speech and language or occupational therapy sessions.

We did attend some of those sorts of things later, with mixed results, but they were never a central part of our programme for helping Daniel and were never anywhere near as valuable or transformative as the approaches we did choose to adopt and focus on. We didn't completely cut them out, we just stopped relying on them – accepted them if they were there and they looked useful, but never felt a dependency on them. We had the same attitude to his official autism diagnosis – we went along with the process, but without any urgency. We didn't attribute much importance to the diagnosis by the time it came round, we just wanted to find a way to support him whatever the name tag was that they wanted to give to his condition. We knew very well by then that he had autism, and more importantly, we had taken serious steps to address his sufferings and help him to develop. Interestingly, having decided to detach ourselves and not expect anything from these authorities, the process went very smoothly and he got his official diagnosis unusually early - shortly before his third birthday, a little over a year after he was first referred to the Community Paediatrician. By that time, we had returned from the Mifne Centre in Israel (of which much more in chapter 3), and his condition was much improved.   The professionals who had first seen him before we went there over the summer of 2011 and who fully expected him to be ranked at the very severe end of the autistic spectrum, were astonished in August 2012 when his assessment placed him at the very mild end. They asked us what we thought could have contributed to this remarkable improvement.   We told them about our trip to Israel and how the clinic we had visited there had used a simple and easy method that is proven to dramatically improve the quality of life of very young autistic children.   They seemed very pleased for us so we offered to tell them more about it and even to put them in contact with the centre, who are always keen to spread their methods to interested carers around the world to help as many children as possible.   But they became less keen at this point, explaining, "No, we have our own way of treating people here."   It was an interesting response, because we hadn't seen any evidence of any meaningful way they had of treating anyone.   It had seemed as if assessment was their principal concern, which culminated in diagnosis, and that after that, there wasn't much to do apart from some token sessions or classes here and there. Even these were far too small in quantity and too general in focus and too overcrowded with thoughtlessly matched children to be able to make any serious difference to any child.   I don't know if this was because there was an underlying assumption that there was nothing very effective that could be done to treat autism, or a recognition that if there was they didn't have the means to achieve it, either in terms of money or of expertise. The reasons were never clear.

A consequence of making that psychological break from depending on the medical system was that our darkest period seemed to end with it. We started seeing small signs of improvement very quickly when we were able to bring more of our own energy and positivity to Daniel and to looking for other ways to treat him, instead of allowing engagement with the medical system to drain us. We discovered how much it had taken out of us relying on doctors and specialists and appointments and assessments and diagnoses, hitting against their reluctance to do anything for us, needing to monitor and push them at every stage to make anything happen, and then being disappointed with the lack of input and results when anything did. It didn't leave us with much in the way of resources to do what our main job was – to help and support our son.

It was actually just a few days before the events just recounted at the end of June 2011 that we started to introduce some private and less mainstream treatments to Daniel. The first was cranial osteopathy, which we still count as one of the best maintenance therapies we have tried. The therapist works using touch and sometimes very gentle massage of the child's head and body, and through doing so understands what is wrong in the body and how to treat it – and Daniel was able to carry on playing with cars or whatever he was doing while being treated. I have never understood how this works and what exactly they perceive and are able to do, but it very clearly made a difference to Daniel, as it has to a lot of children, and it was interesting that he co-operated with the treatment much more than we would have expected. When we first walked into the centre and saw that the other children there were being treated with hands placed on their heads and bodies, we were sure that Daniel would determinedly throw the therapist's hand away, but he didn't. He did wriggle uncomfortably a bit and made his displeasure evident, but didn't actually reject the treatment. We went to the Osteopathic Children's Centre[2] in Putney (they have other locations as well) which is actually where new cranial osteopath's are trained. It is these students who do most of the treatments, but they are closely supervised by very experienced trainers, who often ended up finishing the work with Daniel anyway. This had the advantage that it was inexpensive (there was a suggested charge of £35 per session, but as it was a charity and a training institution, patients could pay more or less than that depending on what they could afford), and the students got to learn, while their trainers ensured that whatever work needed to be completed on the child actually happened.

---

[2] http://occ.uk.com/

After his first session there, he urinated quite profusely for the rest of the morning, despite not having drunk much water, and then went to sleep for a long time. When he woke up, we were very surprised by the calmness and absence of screaming, and then much more so when he began to make better eye-contact with us and to look around with what really looked like more awareness of his surroundings. He displayed some understanding of our attempts to show him things by pointing, and didn't recoil from them. He even seemed a little contented at times. All of this was most marked on the day of the session, but he retained some of it through the week, as well as seeming calmer, having fewer and less intense meltdowns, less self-harm and less staring into space. It was the first week of hope that we had experienced for several months. We took him back the following week, and the therapist was very happy with the changes she perceived in him since the first session (we were told that the treatment received during the sessions initiates a healing response in the body that continues over the following days), however we never got to experience any benefits that would have arisen from this second session, as this was the day of the appointment with the Clinical Paediatrician (related earlier). We actually went directly from the Osteopathy Centre to that appointment, where he was woken from his post-treatment sleep, undressed and sent into a violent meltdown. Following that, and the experience with the CT scan in the Children's Ward a couple of days after it, all of the benefits from the cranial osteopathy, were more than wiped away and there was a period of intense regression. We did return once in July, and the therapist who had treated him previously was very surprised when she felt during the treatment that the progress that had been made had been reversed, and his entire system was extremely tensed up, as if it was retaining colossal stress. Again, there was a distinct improvement after the session – Daniel showed a rare softness and a preference to be around us rather than on his own, better eye-contact and even slightly more articulated consonant sounds rather than his usual slurred grunting sounds. But after his experiences in the hospital, this improvement was from a lower base than it had been the previous month, and so it wasn't very surprising that he was still very unsettled and prone to meltdowns (though usually without self-harm now). Again, these results were retained, but not consistently, and while there were some quite promising signs of the beginnings of some sort of recovery over that summer, there were also periods of deep regression and worrying loss of control of his means of expression. It would have been valuable to have gone to more cranial osteopathy sessions at that time, and we did so more regularly after we returned from our treatment in Israel in November. We still use cranial osteopathy for Daniel now (and sometimes for ourselves) when a stressful incident occurs or when he seems to be going through a difficult time, or when he suffers a major bang, especially to the head. We have found an excellent osteopath, who was actually involved in the setup of the Osteopathic Children's Centre in the 1980s, and who now lives not far from us, and we consistently see real results from a visit to him. For example, while writing this chapter, Daniel was going through a long period of making silly noises all the time in response to whatever we said to him and thinking it to be hilarious. So we took him for an osteopathy session, and the next day, although still enjoying his silliness, was notably less dogmatic about expressing it, and more open to the understanding that it was not as much fun for everyone else as it was for him; and we were able to communicate more effectively with him again. We greatly value this therapy.

If the way cranial osteopathy works is difficult to understand and explain, the fundamentals of radionics, which was the other therapy we experimented with that summer, are much much harder. Had it not been for the recommendation of a friend who knew and highly regarded a particular practitioner of radionics, we would never have come across this therapy, and if we had, we would never have seriously considered it. As it was, we were sceptical. All of the sessions we had were conducted over Skype, and we never met the therapist in person. Some of them were conducted while Daniel was out or asleep. At the first consultation (which was on the day in between the 2 hospital incidents), the therapist offered to explain to us how the "machine" he used to treat people worked. I declined, suspecting that if I knew too much about it, I would be even less inclined to proceed. This was probably a wise move, having already seen his machine (which I seem to remember was very much like an open briefcase with a series of dials and switches, a few apparently randomly placed wires and a space where he needed to put something related to the person being treated - in our case, this was a photograph of Daniel we had sent him). While writing this chapter, I came across an interview with another British practitioner of radionics in which she acknowledged, "Believe me, there's not a single person involved in radionics who hasn't gone into it thinking 'This can't possibly work'."[3] We were given different types of feedback during the sessions concerning what he discovered and what he was treating. Some of it was physical, such as the presence of a virus or the misalignment of a particular bone (which he claimed he could adjust remotely), while some of it was less easily tangible, about energetic fields and auras. In each case, he asked us some questions, then twisted the dials a bit, noted some things down and then told us he had sent a treatment. It didn't seem that anything was happening at all, but interestingly, there were results. After our first session (Daniel was asleep), he woke up a little more alert, looking around the room more (as he had after his osteopathy),

---

[3]

http://www.telegraph.co.uk/lifestyle/wellbeing/5356013/Radionics-can-a-lock-of-hair-hold-the-key-to-health.html articulating sounds slightly better, and most significantly, feeling a little more comfortable around us, less disturbed by our presence near him. This was all the more remarkable after the events at the hospital the previous day, and was, of course, wiped out by the events of the following day. But we had 3 more sessions over the summer. In the days following the next one, he seemed noticeably softer and less uncomfortable around us again, laughing at me once, allowing me to spin him round one time and to hold him briefly another time. These were small isolated episodes, but they were nevertheless unprecedented in our lives at that time, and always seemed to happen in the days following a session. After a session in September, he even seemed to be showing a book and a car to his mother, he made occasional eye contact (on one occasion prolonged), he emptied a drawer of toys onto the floor after months of seeming to have neither the energy nor the interest to do such things, his grunting reduced and he even began to use the word "no" again. So we were very grateful for these changes, but we ended up not continuing with the radionics for very long after we returned from our treatment in Israel that autumn. We were on a different path by that time, which we felt comfortable with. We had noticed that the benefits of the radionics sessions were impressive and significant, but faded quickly after the treatments - sometimes by the next day. The therapist felt that this was due to an underlying issue that he had found and did start to treat it that summer, and had we continued, the results of the sessions may have become more permanent. But we also had another experience of radionics, which was that I had some sessions myself, and found that while I felt some definite relief from the symptoms I had gone with, there were other minor irritations that began. It was explained to me that it sometimes happens in radionics that when one thing is treated, the work has a knóck on effect on something else, which then needs further treatment. We thought that this was fine, but implies more of a long term commitment to the therapy. We were very happy that we had used radionics that summer, but by this time, we had very limited funds, which were being more than absorbed by the costs of the treatment in Israel and the follow on therapy back home, so we felt the need to prioritise.

The only reason we had any funds at all for Daniel's treatments is because we had applied early for Disability Living Allowance and Carers' Allowance, which together came to nearly £500 each month at the time. It sounds like a lot, but it can go so quickly as therapies are so expensive. Some of the horrific experiences we had had with the doctors at least provided evidence of the severity of Daniel's condition, and we were fortunate to come across the charity, Cerebra[4], who had expertise in filling in the applications forms for these allowances. Expertise

---

[4] http://w3.cerebra.org.uk/

was needed, because not only are the forms complicated and not always clear about what exactly they are looking for, but they also appeared to include certain traps that could be used to turn down an application or to award a lower level of payment than would otherwise be due. For example, there are places where they ask for the same information that they have already asked for, but in a completely different way, the apparent intention being to weed out fraudulent claims by inviting contradictions. But the system didn't seem to have the flexibility to understand when a case was genuine but the applicant had just understood the question in a different way and put down apparently inconsistent information. We heard several stories of families in obvious genuine need to support their disabled children who were turned down altogether for these allowances for no easily discernible reason - even when the forms were filled in with support. So we weren't sure that we were going to be awarded anything until official notification came through. The representative from Cerebra came to our home (I think she visited twice) and went through the form with us and our proposed answers. Based on what we had told her about Daniel, she prompted us to include information that better represented our true situation and which we might otherwise have overlooked. Cerebra also funds certain treatments and types of equipment, and they gave us generous grant the following year to fund 2 series of music therapy sessions.

While cranial osteopathy and radionics were having some initially modest but clear and promising results for us that we wanted to build on, we felt that in order to bring about more fundamental and permanent change, we really needed, in addition to them, a more complete and immersive approach to living with Daniel's condition and improving his quality of life, focusing on the underlying attitudes and environment that he was subjected to. The Mifne Centre in Israel really seemed to be the only place we could find that would effectively provide that. We did look at alternatives. One of them was called FloorTime, which although less directive than the Mifne method, shared its approach of treating the child by building a relationship with them, eliciting their trust and showing them that there is much outside themselves which is both safe and fulfilling. Therapists would work with children, either at home or in another agreed place, and one or both parents would also be involved – so they would learn how to apply the principles in daily life. We would probably have investigated this much further had we not gone to Mifne.

Another was the Son-Rise programme[5], which was another method of working with the child in an immersive programme at home. We did look seriously at this, but there were a couple of things that didn't really fit for us.

---

[5] http://www.autismtreatmentcenter.org/

It was a course for parents to learn how to create their own programme to implement for their child at home, but they were expected to go without the child and to learn about it in a classroom/training setting. Not only would that have been logistically difficult, as Daniel really depended on us for childcare at that time and nobody else was really able to manage him without one of us around, but it also felt too abstract for us – we would learn the theory, but not have any true understanding of how it would work with our son until we arrived home and tried it, and then there was a significant risk of it all unravelling as many things didn't work the way we had understood in our ideal theoretical picture. Plus neither of us is very good at learning things via lectures. We were also a little put off by the fact that even though it was a charitable foundation, its marketing felt very much like they had something to sell - listing the benefits of the approach, using sentimental videos and emotive music, sending out glossy materials and DVDs about the course, offering a "free 25 minute call" to ask questions about the programme, and following up any contact with emails and calls to remind us what they had to offer. After the "foundation"course, they had various follow on courses to deepen understanding of aspects of the training (which made us think – perhaps not looking on the bright side - that we therefore probably wouldn't learn all that we needed on the initial course and that it would be a long term commitment with continual issues of logistics and expense). It was based in America (naturally) and so would also have meant that we would be totally separated from Daniel for its entire duration, though they do now seem to offer occasional courses in the UK. These were only our initial impressions based on the limited research that we did on them, and I'm sure we would have investigated further had we not had the opportunity to go to the Mifne Centre. But these are the reasons why, at that time, we were less enthusiastic about this programme.

So there were alternatives, but based on our research and our strong feeling about it, we were actually determined to go to Mifne. It was by far the approach we liked best, and offered easily the best kick start we had come across – a 3 week intensive programme in which Daniel would be exclusively treated by a team of psychotherapists (only one family was treated at any time in the clinic), and in which we, the parents, would be intricately involved in the training in order to learn it and experience how to live by it beyond our visit. It really sounded like a perfectly crafted programme. The problem was that it wasn't up to us to decide whether we would get a place there. They are extremely busy and Daniel was already approaching the upper age limit of children they would treat. Emotionally, we were, perhaps unwisely, putting all our eggs in one basket and would have been both devastated and directionless (at least for a while) if we hadn't been offered a place. We had sent the clinic a full report about Daniel and videos of him showing his condition, but they insisted that in order for them to be able to treat us, an autism diagnosis was required by Israeli law. As it would have been impossible at his age, and at the required speed, to get such a diagnosis in the UK (as in most countries), they agreed instead that we would seek a preliminary diagnosis and a recommendation of treatment at Mifne from one of the specialist child psychotherapists they work with in the UK. So we did go along to the person they recommended, who we later found out to be a prestigious and well-known expert in autism. We didn't feel positive about these sessions, even before we had started - not having come to terms with the expense, and also because of the inconvenience of getting there - it was a 2-hour trek each way across London, with multiple changes of train, tube and bus with an often impatient Daniel in his pushchair, necessitating arrangements to be made with work and so on. We didn't have any particular expectations of the therapy, as it hadn't been our choice to go there, but we did like the therapist and she seemed to understand Daniel and gave us some useful insights and ideas. Critically, she gave us the diagnosis we needed in order to be able to be treated at Mifne, and wrote them a full report about all of her observations of Daniel and our family.

Soon after this, we were invited to Israel for treatment at the clinic, and a new phase of our lives began; one that was characterised by positivity and hope.

Chapter 3 - The Turning Point

Driving in early October 2011 from Tel-Aviv, where we had landed, to the village of Rosh Pinna in the north of Israel, I remember wondering whether we would actually find a   clinic there at all, or whether the "small deposit" of £2,000 that we had paid prior to arrival was the main goal of what now seemed like the meagre level of communication we had had with them at that time. Fortunately, my worries were unfounded.

The vast majority of people reading this will never get a chance to visit the Mifne Centre[6], as it now works exclusively with children under 2 years old, and it is extremely unlikely in the UK, as in most countries, for autism to be identified and diagnosed early enough for parents to make preparations for a visit there before the

---

[6] http://mifne-autism.com/

child's second birthday. However, I am going to write at some length about our experiences there, as they form the crux of how Daniel's life was improved and how we continued his treatment when we returned home. We learnt so many very simple and in retrospect self-evident attitudes and ways of being that have truly changed our lives, and which I have no doubt could be transformative to many other families as well, with a little perseverance. The underlying principles are not age-specific and are relevant to all. Of course, this chapter is not intended as a guide or a set of instructions to any family looking to establish a programme of therapy for their children, nor is it an attempt to represent the philosophy or structure of the Mifne Centre, but I hope it can give some ideas and inspiration to other families, along with a deeper realisation that their children are not beyond reach or beyond hope. It may even provide a better understanding of the real potential within them, as well as a starting point for how to respect and nurture that potential. Of course, reading about such things and trying to act on the insights they bring without recourse to support is not the same as actually being at a state-of-the-art specialist clinic, watching treatments through a glass mirror for hours every day, analysing what is happening and how best to respond to it with the help of extremely competent trainers, trying it out ourselves while being observed by them and getting continual incisive feedback on what worked and didn't, and on how to refine our behaviour towards our son. But even reading about them can give a very good starting point on which to base changed attitudes and behaviours to yield significant results. In order to supplement what is in this book, I have set up a blog[7] (which can be found at http://transformingautism.co.uk), with a mission to redefine autism, understand the true inner nature of autistic individuals and thereby support parents and carers of autistic people to better support them. It will include posts related to the subject matter of this book, and will use the comments that readers and other visitors leave as a way to understand what additional content would be most useful to provide.

The summer of 2011 had been turbulent, as you have read. Having started on cranial osteopathy and radionics, we had seen some periods of great hope, but these were often succeeded by periods of further regression, and the trip to Israel itself had been difficult for him. He hadn't wanted to let go of his pushchair (which we had had to hand over to the cabin staff when we reached the plane) or to get into the plane through the door, and needed to be held, first screaming and then sleeping, for the entire journey. We wondered whether we were doing the right thing by going there, or whether we had recklessly compounded his anxiety for a desperate hope of something impossible. For a while, we also wondered whether we

---

[7] http://transformingautism.co.uk

would be asked to leave the plane due to the loud screaming right from before we boarded, but we weren't. We had deliberately gone slightly early and booked a few days at a hotel in Tel Aviv near the beach in advance of the treatment. We hadn't had a family holiday before, and we had hopes even of paddling together in the sea. But, perhaps because of the heat or the unfamiliar surroundings or just the particular phase he was going through at that time, Daniel seemed extremely unhappy there, and we barely left the hotel with him, except to push him around in the pushchair. Instead we took it in turns to go out and get food or have the odd hour in the sea.

When we arrived in Rosh Pinna, where the Mifne Centre was situated (Mifne means *turning point* in Hebrew), the place we were put up in turned out to be a quite luxurious house a few minutes' walk up a steep hill to the clinic. When we arrived, Daniel was sleeping in his car seat, which we lifted out of the car and put in the lounge so that he could wake up naturally when he was ready, while we unpacked our cases. While he was still sleeping, we received a visit from a man and a woman, who welcomed us very warmly. They were actually the 2 therapists who were going to lead Daniel's programme, though we didn't realise this at the time. We assumed that the warm welcome was just Israeli hospitality, which it may well have been, in part, but we understood later that it was also integral to the Mifne approach. While we had gone there thinking that the treatment would be for Daniel, they actually saw each treatment as a whole family affair. We were not only intricately involved in the Daniel's autism treatment itself - effectively being intensively trained to continue it once we returned home - we were also subject to various types of therapy ourselves in order to remove any baggage we were carrying that might impact our approach to parenting. And we were carefully looked after for our whole time there, as the staff there did all they could to treat us well, make sure we had breaks and time to spend together, and to alleviate the enormous stress that we were clearly shouldering from the situation of the past year or so. The thinking was that if we were full of anxiety and fatigue, there would be a limited amount we would be able to bring to helping improving Daniel's quality of life.

When Daniel did wake up in his car seat in the lounge, he was uncharacteristically happy. He stepped out of the seat, took one of each of our hands and seemed to want to go out for a walk. We were surprised and pleased by this, and went out together to the porch at the front, where the pushchair was still folded, ready to open it up for him to sit in. But for the first time we could remember, he just stepped over it, not seeming to even notice it. It was a one-off and he demanded it again the next morning, but it was unprecedented and we weren't sure what was happening. We actually never did find an explanation for this unusually positive behaviour, which continued into the next day when our treatment started.

That morning we pushed Daniel up the hill in his pushchair ready to start, but with no idea what would happen. We were given a brief introduction to the Centre – it was a large and beautifully located building at the foot of some cliffs. There was a team of 6 therapists and the Director of the Centre, Dr. Hanna Alonim, one of the warmest and most impressive people we have ever met. She would lead Daniel's programme, but would never actually meet him in person until the end of it. We were the only family being treated there – they treat only one family at a time – and we felt quite honoured to have the whole centre and its staff dedicated to our family's treatment for a full 3 weeks. Then, the three of us were sent along with one of the therapists to a large but almost empty room, which turned out to be the therapy room where Daniel would spend around 7 hours a day, 7 days a week for the next 3 weeks. There were a couple of shelves with a few boxes of toys on them, and a bathroom area adjoined through a door where there was a large cupboard with more boxes of toys in it, but there was very little within reach in the room itself, apart from some soft toy steps & slide, and a large wooden train on wheels that could be climbed into and moved around. There was a large one-way mirror, on the other side of which was an observation room, where we would sit for much of the time during our stay, watching the therapy through the glass, making notes on it and filling in questionnaires designed to deepen our understanding of what we were seeing. The proceedings in the room were also filmed and streamed to television screens across the building, so that we and the team of therapists supporting us could keep an eye on the evolving situation and on any progress while we were busy with other things.

Once in the room, Daniel became very interested in the toys there, playing and exploring for quite some time. We wondered where he had found this new enthusiasm for life, and right after his spontaneous wish to go for a walk the night before. We feared that the team there would think we had been exaggerating Daniel's condition and wasting their time when they could have been helping someone in real need. We were each taken out individually and spoken to by different therapists while watching Daniel on a screen. We were each asked whether we were surprised by Daniel's keen interest in the items in the room and whether it reflected his usual behaviour at home. We each said no. We were told that if he was displaying such interest in toys now, he can't have been as cut off from the world as we had claimed in all our correspondence. We each felt that we were being reprimanded and accused of fabricating the severity of Daniel's issues, and we each became a little defensive. But the intention had not been to confront us. Of course, despite the positive beginning, they could still clearly see that he was autistic, and there was little or no attempt by him to interact with anybody else.   Rather, it had been to get us to understand that whatever we had observed in Daniel back in England, he had far more potential to enjoy life than we could have suspected, and much more even than what we were seeing now.   At that point, we had no idea what to do with that understanding, but that was what the next 3 weeks would be about – for us to learn to recognise, appreciate and nurture his potential so that we could support his growth and development.

When we were both back in the therapy room, it was time for the first shock.   We were both to leave the room at the same time, and leave him with the therapists there[8].   Until that moment, apart from very brief periods with his grandparents, he had never been apart from both of us.   It was a challenge for us as well as for Daniel, and we were very apprehensive.   We didn't know whether he would go into meltdown or not react at all.   In the event he didn't show any emotional reaction, but his interest in the toys immediately stopped, and he walked over to lie down passively by the door that we had just walked out of. He stayed there for some considerable time and we felt terrible.

---

[8] To the best of my recollection, this separation took place on the first day, though the records that Mifne keep state that it was the third.   Therefore, the exact sequence of events might have been slightly different to what is recounted here, but the gist of our learning is accurately represented.

But this was only his first challenge, because while we were out of the room, we were taken to an office and given our first practical advice about managing Daniel during his time there and beyond. This came in the form of our first piece of homework, which was to fold down the pushchair and put it away until the treatment finished 3 weeks later, requiring him to walk everywhere. It was about starting to give him a structure in his life and providing a sense of order and security, but doing so with love, leaving him in no doubt that we were on his side throughout. We were told that parents of children with special needs were very often highly over-protective of them, indulging their demands and failing to effectively provide this sense of order effectively out of a fear that it would lead to meltdowns, a constant state of anxiety and eventual alienation in an already challenged child. Basically, we get frightened that they will not be able to cope with being given limits and that this would make their condition worse, so we let them have what they demand. But the actual result of doing this is that they never learn to cope with the adversity that life is likely to present them with on a regular basis – they just get used to having what they believe they need (even if they don't), and their need for it solidifies, so they never develop independence. It is certainly true that they already have plenty of adversity to contend with without having their basic crutches (like the pushchair) taken away from them, but weaning them off these crutches, done sensitively, with care that the need being addressed through them is fulfilled in other ways, can actually empower them to grow and develop and gives them a reassurance that they can cope with situations without falling back on them. But *how* to do this sensitively? Going straight in, determinedly laying down the law and just taking away the pushchair or anything else, oblivious to their screams of protest, probably *would* lead to increasing alienation and regression in the child. This is where the concept of discipline with love came in. We realised on that day how rarely we had ever seen this practised, and how the concepts of discipline and love are commonly treated as mutually exclusive – "love" being understood as a soft and happy condition with a sense of deep connection, and "discipline" as a demand, often delivered in a warning tone, with an implicit threat of conflict if it is not adhered to. It is rare to see these concepts brought together into a single positive interaction. And there wasn't any magical secret to it; it was simply a case of telling Daniel how things were going to be, but then rather than demanding compliance, just staying with him as a good friend and giving him the loving support he needed to help him through the transition. We were not to demand anything from him, but rather to let him know what was going to happen and then patiently, confidently and with love reassure him that this was fine and that he could easily cope with the new situation, helping him with any emotional upset that the change might generate. The change itself was not negotiable, but there was no need to become his enemy in the course of its implementation.

When we did put the pushchair away that evening, there wasn't much protest, because it was our first real evening there, and he didn't realise that the pushchair wasn't going to be put away every evening and then retrieved the following morning to go out. The problem came in the morning, when we needed to walk up the hill to the Centre for our second day of treatment. As we went to the door without the pushchair, alarm registered in his face and he threw himself on the floor in demand for it, expecting us to get it for him as we usually did. But this time, we did what we'd been told – we stayed very calm, with no sense that there was a "situation" of any sort. We lifted him up and held him warmly and softly explained that we were going without the pushchair today and that this was fine and that he was big and strong enough to walk. We were ready to stay with him and support him as long as he needed for him to calm down – we had allowed plenty of extra time to accommodate this, and the therapy team also knew what we were doing and so would not be surprised if it took even longer than we anticipated. There was a long period of screaming, but the constant warm and unflustered reassurance we were giving him that we would all easily be able to manage going up the hill without the pushchair seemed gradually to have an effect on him, and he did reluctantly come with us – snivelling and unhappy, but willingly. He stopped to protest several times along the way – or moved in front of us and raised his arms to let us know he expected to be carried – but each time, we stopped walking, lifted him up again and warmly reassured him that he could walk. Eventually he did. As we got close to the Centre, he had one final intense protest, lying down, screaming and refusing to move. We kneeled down to his level and continued to reassure him that everything was fine, that he had done really well and we were proud of him, and that we were almost there. This time, it didn't make much difference, and for a while we thought that we might possibly give up and carry him the final steps. An elderly woman passing by made clear to us that she thought we were being cruel to our child by not giving him what he wanted (though she seemed less outraged when we told her we were being treated in the Mifne Centre and they had instructed us to do this). We decided to stay with it, and eventually he did co-operate, taking our hands again to make it to the Centre, very late. All the way there, we congratulated him on his bravery, and the affirmation seemed to have some impact on him, even though he wouldn't have understood the words themselves. The team were similarly celebratory when he arrived there, so his overall experience was that despite the difficulty of accepting this new reality, he had achieved something and was surrounded by positivity about it. Importantly, he got the message that however impossible it had initially seemed, he had made it through to the end – with constant support from his parents - and that in doing so, had earned approval and acclaim from others. As the days passed, the walks up the hill became gradually easier and less fraught. By the second week, he was sobbing and blubbering all the way (rather than screaming and protesting), but still walking determinedly up the hill holding each of our hands - I remember proudly telling him on one such day as we were walking up that he was walking bravely like a soldier, and he seemed to appreciate the sentiment.

But back on that first day, in the office, the prospect of taking away his pushchair seemed cruel and daunting. We agreed to it, and trusted their advice, but were very nervous about how it would go. We also discussed what else we had been doing in an over-protective vein that might have impeded Daniel's ability to have confidence in the world and in himself, and to become independent and develop as a child would normally be expected to. Clearly, there was the dependence on the pushchair for movement and for sleeping, but there were many more things. Perhaps the biggest was around food, where we had accepted his refusal to eat by himself and allowed him to eat at his own pace, being spoon-fed at a rate he decided in front of cartoons of his choice. It had seemed like the only possible way to get him to eat anything at all, but we would learn a new approach to food issues that we would implement with great success while we were there and later on. We had also been letting him sleep as long as he wanted in the afternoons and in the environment that he demanded (because he believed he needed it and we had bought into that belief). Often he was sleeping for 3 to 4 hours. They explained to us that an hour is ideal, and an hour and a half was the maximum that should be allowed for an afternoon sleep, as more than that would mean he went to a deeper level of sleep and woke up more disoriented and less able to engage with the world for a long time (indeed, he had often just stared out blankly for a long time after his afternoon sleeps). But we had been afraid of waking him before he was ready, fearing unnecessary meltdowns. In the therapy room, there was no pushchair to sleep in. He was made a simple bed on the floor when he was starting to look tired, and he had the option to sleep on that, which he willingly did when he was tired enough. He was gently woken after an hour. It worked very well, but at that time, on our first day, we hadn't seen any of it yet and all of this was still theory. It felt like it was going to be a very hard 3 weeks. Perhaps the most damaging thing we had been doing that had robbed him of his ability to become independent was more subtle – it was in our own emotional state when there were any issues or potential issues. For example, we had often experienced fear that he might go into meltdown when things were going wrong, or had felt a tense uncertainty and anxiety whenever a "situation" looked like it was beginning. We hadn't realised that this in itself could fuel problems. But we would learn much more about how that piece worked the following day.

When we left the office, we went up to the observation room, and saw an astonishing and very welcome sight. Daniel was sitting at a small table with a tray of solid food in front of him, and feeding himself with a fork. We hadn't dared hope that he would achieve this even by the end of our treatment, but this was the very first day, barely 3 hours after our arrival. Their attitude to food was another instance of transferring responsibility back to the child. The child would be offered food on the adults' terms – at a seat at a table for a fixed length of time – and if they chose not to eat it in that way or within that time, they would need to wait for the next meal. They would be offered simple light snacks in between, like fresh fruit, so that they didn't starve, but not enough for them to feel satisfied enough to keep skipping meals. The thinking was that each child has a natural survival instinct and, in normal circumstances, this is what drives them to eat. When Daniel was refusing food and we were giving it to him on his terms – in front of cartoons, being spoon fed to him – we were bypassing that natural survival instinct and assuming responsibility for his eating ourselves. He was eating for us, and had no incentive to even think about food himself. When it came to food, we had been treating our 2 year old child like a 2 month old baby. The transition, we were told, was not always easy, and so it proved with Daniel. After the fluke of the initial meal (which we still can't explain – just as we can't explain the walking without his pushchair on the first evening or the sudden playing with the toys on arrival at the clinic), there was a lot of fussiness and resistance around food during much of the trip and beyond, and we needed to implement this strategy without any hint of emotion or impatience or disappointment or anxiety. We needed to simply keep offering and accepting his decision with trust in him that he would not let himself starve. It did work. We didn't get to the ideal state where there was no fussiness and no refusals, but on balance, over the course of any week, we could see that he was actually eating as much as he needed, even if there may have been periods within that week when he seemed to be eating worryingly little. They told us that in all their 25 years of treating children with autism, none had ever allowed themselves to get to a critical state before taking responsibility for their eating, though there had been one extreme case in which a girl had barely eaten anything for 10 days and they had been getting very worried about her, but the approach was eventually successful even with her in the end.

The first day had been a revelation, but it was on the second that we learnt from Hanna, the Director of the Mifne Centre, perhaps the most important concept of our stay, and one that we have been implementing as best we can even since. After our long and difficult walk up the hill on that day (that I have described) we – and especially

Daniel – were warmly greeted at the clinic, and again we all went up to the therapy room together. Daniel enjoyed half an hour of exploring the room with us around him until we were asked to leave again and a therapist would take over. Again, Daniel showed no emotion to see us go, but seemed to switch off as soon as we left, and went to lie on the floor near the door. This is where he spent much of his time during our stay. He would lie there as soon as we both left him, and show no interest for a long time in what the therapists were doing. When they did eventually find a way to recapture his imagination and he did briefly engage with whatever activity they were offering him, this would last a certain amount of time and then he would break off, presumably becoming once again conscious of his unhappiness, and resume his place by the door. It was very hard and painful to watch this, but we understood, and can understand better now, that it was part of his process of breaking the inappropriate level of his dependence on us, that was one of the factors impeding his development. Critically, he was never made to feel abandoned, and whenever we left him we gave him warm reassurances that we would be back soon and he was going to have a really nice time with the therapists, and they were unfailingly warm and inviting to him however much he may have ignored their invitations. At first, he failed to register us when we got back – as if he had been hurt by having been left, but as time went on, he showed more "appropriate" emotions both when we left and when we returned. When we left, he started to cry for a while and allowed himself to be comforted by the therapist there, rather than internalising his sadness and cutting off from his environment and lying inert by the door. When we returned, he started to show some joy to see us. From the start, the whole process of separation – actually the first in his life – was very interesting for us as well as painful. After many months of having little or no indication that he valued our being around - or even registered it - it was a shock to see how much our absence was affecting him. It was clearly critically important for him that we were around, even though he had never expressed this, and it was another reminder of how much goes on inside the mind and heart of an autistic child that finds no expression, leading others, even their closest family, to assume that there is a vacuum rather than the immense richness of feeling that is actually there.

When we left the therapy room, we were asked to go to Hanna's office, where she presented to us for the first time the concept of "containment". It was a deceptively simple idea, but the impact of implementing it was absolutely critical to the success of any of the approaches we learnt at Mifne (and arguably any approach at all). We were asked first of all to imagine Daniel's environment as being represented by a box. He was inside the box, and we, as his parents and carers, largely comprised the walls of the box. Our job was simply to keep him contained within the box, so that he felt secure and free in his environment. Whenever anything went wrong around him, that represented to him a threat to his environment and he would feel a terror that the walls of his box would give way, leaving him exposed to whatever horrors might be on the other side. We had to help him to understand and believe that everything was fine and that the wrong thing that had happened wasn't really so bad and could be easily dealt with. If we did that successfully, he would again feel secure in his environment, and if we did it consistently, he would eventually learn to calm and settle himself in difficult situations. If we failed, he would experience the event as if the walls of the box were crumbling, and if we failed consistently, he would come to understand his environment as an unsafe, unstable place that was not to be trusted, and that he was constantly under threat of annihilation. It may sound a little strange or abstract, but it is simply a way of representing his perceived vulnerability and the importance of our role in making him feel safe. It has proved an incredibly useful reference for us in the years since Hanna explained it to us. All it means in practice is that we need to consistently behave in a way that assures him that, whatever happens, everything is okay. But how to do this? It is not as simple as just saying the words, "it's okay" whenever there is a problem. This could easily become a lazy cliché, and like many intuitive children, especially autistic children, he would naturally understand whether we really meant what we said and whether there was any discrepancy between our words and what we were actually feeling about whatever was going on. This was not about learning any technique to use to make Daniel feel how we wanted him to feel; this was much more fundamental, and involved managing our own feelings and condition as much of the time as possible. The only way Daniel could be calmed when in a state of unease or distress was for the people around him to be in a contrasting state; not only believing that the situation would turn out for the best, but also absolutely trusting that Daniel himself would be fine. That's why any feeding issues needed to be handled without emotion or anxiety on our part, because if, while we were trying to "manage" the situation, the commentary going through our own minds was anything like, "Oh God, not this again. I don't know how we're going to get him to eat. This is a real problem," this would necessarily be reflected in our behaviour in subtle ways, which Daniel would easily be able to pick up on. And when he did, the message he would take from it would be something like, "There is a problem here. The people who I trust and depend on (and who represent the walls of my box) feel anxious, and if *they* feel anxious, there must be something to feel anxious about. Now I'm really scared." And fear can lead to meltdowns, or to stored anxiety that will mean bigger meltdowns more easily triggered later. We all know that there is not much to do about meltdowns once they start, but we found that containing Daniel could avert meltdowns from starting in the first place. We had seen a good model of this the previous day during Daniel's first meal. At one point, he moved his arm quickly and knocked his cup of drink flying across the table and all over the floor. In other circumstances, this might have led to one of us rushing unhappily to clean it up as quickly as possible, or at least sighing unhappily. We would have thought of such a reaction as being an unremarkable expression of how we were feeling, but here we were learning that far from being unremarkable, there was colossal power in how we reacted to things, not only in our behaviour, but also in our unspoken thoughts and attitudes. Any hint of negativity on our part would have given him the clear message that there was something wrong (otherwise why would *we* be flustered?) and that this was not a situation in which he could remain calm and relaxed as he was under threat of something terrible; and his anxiety would be unleashed. We had a choice: we could either notice what we were contributing to him with our subtle reactions and work to cultivate self-awareness, positivity and moderation in all of our interactions in order to give Daniel a growing sense of security, or we could choose to continue to assert our right to the uncensored thoughts and reactions that we were entitled to, and probably, more often than not, fuel his inherent anxiety, stalling his development. There was no middle ground. We were starting to understand what level of responsibility we had and how profoundly we were going to need to change ourselves from the inside in order to carry it out. The therapist who was with Daniel when the cup fell simply looked blankly at him, and uttered a playful, "oopa" as a light commentary on what had happened. Daniel seemed quietly contented. When the moment had passed, she could casually reach down and clean up without any gravity.

This is also why it had eventually been effective how we had learnt to handle his walk up the hill without the pushchair from that morning, and why it had led to a greater capacity for independence on his part rather than deeper anxiety and entrenchment, as it could so easily have done if managed differently. We had been told to be very careful to stay light in our being and to remember that everything was fine, whatever happened, so that he could be influenced by this inner attitude of ours. So whenever anything went wrong, or Daniel appeared to be heading towards meltdown or having a wobble about his walk up the hill, we lifted him up calmly and confidently, with a positive attitude and an inner assurance that there was no real issue here, and explained gently, supportively and with conviction that this was how we were going to go to the Centre and that we knew he could cope perfectly well with this. We had chosen to have real patience, and this had profoundly affected him. While it was still necessarily a difficult walk, we started to understand that this was not because he had autism, but because he was used to getting what he demanded. Of course, it was the issues created by autism that had led us all down the path where it was usually the case that he got what he demanded, and that this is a common situation in families with children with disabilities, but we were learning that this wasn't the only necessary outcome, and that we had choices. More importantly, we were starting to see what those choices were and how to make them effectively.

There was a similar situation a little later in the programme that illustrates containment further. There was a shopping centre about 20 minutes' walk from where we were staying (we were getting used to taking longer walks as a family), where Daniel liked to go because there was a large escalator there. He was extremely happy to be going up and down it again and again, and we were delighted to have found something that would give him so much pleasure. As soon as the escalator was in sight (and sometimes well before that), he would yank whichever hand he was holding and determinedly pull us over to it. The problem came when it was time to leave. Daniel could have spent hours going up and down the escalator, so at some point, we needed to lead him away from it. Whenever that point came, there was a meltdown. We weren't sure how to handle this, so we asked one of the therapists. She told us to pick him up and gently tell him, shortly before it was time to finish, that we would be going up and down once more and that we would then leave the area. That evening, I went with Daniel to the shopping centre, and did just that. I picked him up and explained to him that we would be going after the next round on the escalator, though he didn't really seem to be hearing me. As we were coming down for the final time, I reminded him that we were going to leave when we got to the bottom, and when we got there, I took his hand and led him away. Remarkably, he came with me without resistance. After a few steps, he tried to pull me back as he turned to look at the escalators and moaned a bit (as if he was actually considering whether or not to get distressed), but when I gently said, "Come on. Time to go," he came with me without any further issue. I was happy about the result, but couldn't fully understand how it had worked. Not only had Daniel not seemed to be listening to me when I had explained that we were going to leave soon, but even if he had listened, he wouldn't have understood the meaning of what I said. So how could an explanation that he had neither listened to nor understood have proved so effective? I asked the therapist the next day. She told me that simply by picking him up and saying something clearly and calmly to him, this was effectively signalling to him that something might change soon, so it didn't come as such a shock when it did. But more importantly, she asked me how I had felt while explaining to him that we were going to go, and then while leaving the escalator. Had I felt clear and firm in my intention to leave after the next round, and had I felt confident that it would go smoothly and did I trust that it would be fine for Daniel and that I would be able to effectively give him any support he needed in order to get through it easily? Or had I felt uncertain about whether it would be possible and apprehensive about how it would go and fearful that there might be a meltdown and unsure how I might handle it? I told her it was the former, and she said that this condition would have been intuitively perceived by Daniel and it would have given him the reassurance and confidence to trust me and therefore feel safe in his "box". This was containment in action, and it contrasted with our earlier visits to the shopping centre when we would have had more of the other condition, which would similarly have been intuitively perceived by him, and would have led him to his own fear and anxiety that if his carers felt anxious, then there was obviously something to be anxious about. He needed to understand that we were clear and sure that we knew the right thing to do next, and that we could achieve it smoothly without any hint of difficulty, uncertainty or stress. The only way to give him that understanding was to live that condition ourselves.

Learning to contain Daniel through watching the Mifne therapists, as well as being contained by them ourselves as much as possible, was completely transforming our relationship with our son. Family meals became a reality for the first time, and were relaxed and happy rather than full of routine, misery and anxiety. Daniel would even excitedly join us in playing chasing games around the house, and clearly derived huge pleasure from these. We went for family walks together and spent time in the nearby playgrounds. One evening, Oksana and I were sitting on one end of a sea-saw to lift Daniel up high on the other end, and we started singing gently to him. For the first time we could ever remember, he stared directly at us with a beautiful innocent curiosity as if trying to make sense of something enchanting. Things were changing, and it required constant vigilance and self-awareness on our part to ensure that we weren't passively influencing him with any negative thoughts and emotions. We had to learn to notice when these were arising in us and to be strong-willed in dealing with them. It required us to search thoroughly within to find out what was motivating or driving us. Were we feeling worried when he was not engaging or doubting that we had what it took to appeal to him, or fearing that this was all going to unravel? On close inspection of ourselves, it was possible to see that these sorts of emotions could easily come up within us, and so subtly that they would normally have been missed. But they would still have had a profound effect on Daniel. He would have sensed on some level what we were feeling and not only absorbed the negative sentiment, but also taken it to be his truth – that we *didn't* have what it took to appeal to him, and this probably *was* all going to unravel. Having observed them within ourselves, it would have been counter-productive to simply try to wish such feelings away, or artificially replace them with superficial positive thoughts. The only way to manage them effectively was to take a moment to compose ourselves, accept without judgement what had happened, and tune into how we would *like to* be able to feel in any situation; to focus on that and to let it grow. This process, together with the results that we were consistently seeing in Daniel during our stay there, made it easier.

What we were learning about containment also affirmed a decision that we had made long before going to Mifne, that we would not discuss Daniel's condition in front of him. Even though he was unable to understand verbally what was said about him, we both had a feeling that exposing him to situations and conversations where he was discussed as someone who had "a problem" could have a negative effect on him. What we were learning about containment went some way to explaining how that was correct.

Containment formed the backbone of the therapy that Daniel was getting at the Centre. This was natural, as we were encouraged not to see much of a dividing line between the therapy that took place in the therapy room for 6-7 hours each day, and life outside the room. The principles of the therapy were designed to be a permanent enhancement of Daniel's life, and indeed we are still now very much informed by them even though we no longer do the formal play sessions. The room itself was large, but sparse, and the empty space felt refreshing - there was no clutter to distract his attention. Any toys or playing materials were either on shelves high on the wall or in cupboards in the adjoining room - both out of Daniel's reach. This had a dual purpose of countering any tendency he might have had to play on his own while ignoring the therapist who was working with him, and also to require him to communicate clearly to the therapist if he wanted something. This was something we learnt to insist on. Daniel's tendency had been to try to get something he wanted with as little direct communication as possible. When he wanted a toy from a shelf, for example, he would grunt and look at it, without making any eye-contact or other acknowledgement of the person who was with him. If that failed, he might keep his eye fixed on the toy and grab the person's hand and pull them towards the shelf with a grunt as an indication that he wanted something, relying on us to work out, either intuitively or through watching him, to know which item he was looking at and to fulfil his requirement. We were encouraged to try to insist on more direct communication, even by pretending not to understand what he wanted if necessary, forcing him at least to point, and perhaps even to look at us as a means of acknowledging us and establishing he required something from us. However, eye-contact itself was a deeper issue and took much longer, and we didn't push for this or insist on it. Back in England, we had occasionally asked him to "look at me" and he had done so very briefly and for a short and painfully uncomfortable moment, and then looked swiftly away. It was easy to interpret his discomfort and his breaking of eye-contact as a form of rejection – however much we knew it wasn't. We hadn't fully understood at that time, but it was clearly an overwhelming experience for him to look at another person in the eye, and extremely difficult. He was never able to hold eye-contact for more than about half a second at a time. He would have felt perhaps as vulnerable and exposed during that half a second as we would feel if we were in a job interview or on a bus naked. His turning away from us was a manifestation of this extreme discomfort, and not at all a verdict on us. Later, we could see that he might be feeling very connected with us, but still minimise eye-contact. As the therapy progressed and there were times when occasionally he started to enjoy the play, he lost his inhibitions and briefly made quite natural eye-contact for a while (sometimes then becoming conscious of it and retreating). We learnt that the best way to encourage eye-contact was not to draw attention to it at all or even expect it, but to create a more alluring environment around him where his natural propensity to interact freely was encouraged and expanded. Nevertheless, although Daniel's eye-contact improved considerably during our time in Mifne and since, and is now very natural in many situations, it has still not quite reached what would be regarded as normal levels. His school reported to us that for a while they thought he was not paying attention at all, as he didn't look at the teachers when they spoke or were giving instructions, but when they checked in with him and asked him questions, it was clear that he had absorbed everything. So we don't make an issue of eye-contact at all, as we want to avoid creating emotional baggage around it, which would inevitably prove counter-productive. Instead, we do what we can to continue to create an environment for him that he feels he wants to be a part of and interact with. And if there are any related difficulties, for example if he is speaking to someone while looking in the other direction, we never ask him to look at us when he is talking to us (a deeply overwhelming concept which would undoubtedly induce negative feelings), rather we ask him to speak towards our ear so we can hear. The result is the same, but this avoids giving him unnecessary anxiety. If he looks to the side of our face while speaking to us, we now recognise that this is not a problem, and that for him even this is a big and positive step, demonstrating connection with us.

Therapy took place in the room for 6-7 hours each day of our stay, and for most of the time, there was one therapist with Daniel at any time. A therapist would stay with him for about an hour, and then there would be a knock at the door, and another therapist would come in (this therapist would have been watching through the glass and so would know what point she was taking over from). The 2 therapists would greet each other and interact briefly about what had been going on in the play with Daniel in a way that was as inclusive of him as possible, and inviting him to participate in the conversation, but not requiring him to. Then the first therapist would say a warm goodbye and leave the room. This was so that Daniel would get used to being around different people and so that he would learn to feel comfortable with changes. It may have been a little bewildering for him at first to have a succession of different therapists coming in and out of the room, but by the end of our time there, he was quite excited when he heard a knock at the door, and would happily go to answer it to see who it was. The short slots were also for the benefit of the therapy. Working in the room requires constant alertness, emotional availability and responsiveness, warmth and sound judgement that. It would have been difficult to sustain this for much longer periods. There were 6 therapists looking after Daniel, but they were brought in slowly over the initial days. We could watch them through the glass and fill in questionnaires on how they were managing the session, which we could then discuss with them. Other times, we had a go ourselves, putting into practice what we had learnt, on which we received detailed feedback afterwards, so that we could better assimilate how best to help him. After all, when we went back to England, it would be us who would be leading his continuing programme there.

Much of the time in the room was spent improvising

around the various games and props and activities in there, watching for any sign of interest that Daniel showed in anything and building on that. But it wasn't only about waiting for him to decide that he wanted to do something, because so much of the time he was simply staring into space or lying passively by the door, and if the therapist had waited for his lead, it would only have left him free to go deeper into his introspection. So he was continually invited to join in activities. The therapist was there to be with him, and displayed an evident warm wish to play with him. If he was unengaged, she might take something that she knew he liked – like a particular toy or a book – and start playing with it or reading it by herself. She would then start commentating, calmly and sparingly, to him on what she was doing as a way of inviting him in. Surprisingly often, this quickly resulted in Daniel first tilting his head to listen, then discreetly looking round to see what was happening, and eventually going over to the therapist to join her. This was eye-opening for us. It showed us that while we had been bewailing Daniel's increasing staring into space over the summer, we had failed to understand that all it would take to get him to willingly interact with us of his own free will was to keep inviting him to join us in fun activities in a quiet and calm environment. Of course, it was critically important to do this without any emotion (apart from open quiet happiness), or any implicit expectation, and especially not to feel any disappointment if he didn't join us in any activity, as this would have shattered his trust in us and reduced the chances of him accepting any future invitations to participate. He, like many autistic children, is especially intuitive, and the slightest change in our condition could be detected by him and reacted to, sometimes before even we were aware of it ourselves. If he had felt that we expected a particular response from him and that any failure on his part to provide it had been disappointing to us, then he would have felt over-burdened by this unnecessary and heavy responsibility.

There was one especially nice moment when Oksana was moving the pieces of the soft toy slide around and inviting Daniel to join her, but with no response. She made a square in the middle, like a little den, that she could hide in, and waved goodbye to Daniel, who was still sitting on the floor and staring into space in the other direction apparently impervious, and she hid down in the square. His head turned almost imperceptibly to the right, as if he might have been focusing on something, and nothing happened for a while. After a few seconds, Oksana popped up again so he could see her over the top of the den, and gave a joyful hello. Suddenly Daniel turned to her with a big smile on his face, got up and went straight to join her in the square. This sort of thing did not happen every time, but it was enlightening when it did, in the sense that we were seeing the potential to play happily with our son for the first time since his symptoms had become apparent nearly a year earlier. When it didn't happen, we stayed very positive and just kept offering without expectation or disappointment.

Having successfully started to engage with him, we then needed to be very alert to signs of what he was or wasn't interested in and how he was reacting emotionally to the activities. It wasn't unusual – in fact it was a bit of a theme of our time there – for Daniel to suddenly disengage for no apparent reason from an activity that he had been enjoying. Together with the therapists, we tried to understand what was going on. We eventually came to the conclusion that he was simply catching himself opening up and feeling vulnerable about it, and so retreating back to the safer place he was used to. It was important for us to be able to identify when this was happening and to give him some space. Subtly (through our attitude) we could give him the message that it was fine for him to take some time out and, again, that there were no expectations on him. After a suitable pause during which we might be preparing the next activity or even just taking some time out for ourselves, we could start inviting him to something else.

So, while it was true that we were to be very responsive to the indications that Daniel was giving us about what he was enjoying and to build on them, it was also very important for us to have ideas for things we could invite him to next. It might be something as simple as dropping small balls into a pot (which he seemed to like) or spontaneous ideas like putting feathers in each other's hair, or a peek-a-boo game, perhaps with a toy animal involved, or it could be a bigger activity like painting or making something out of clay together or exploring musical instruments. Sometimes, if Daniel seemed responsive to it, it could be more intimate play, like making playful sounds in each other's ear, or tipping him upside down or round and round. As long as we came to each session with enough ideas, and were flexible enough to select which of these ideas to propose based on what mood he was in and whether he showed interest in them, there would be no problem with having something to do together, and never any awkwardness or sense of "what do I do now?". We would have something up our sleeve to suggest to him if he detached from what we were doing. Through doing this, we would be giving him the reassurance that we knew what should happen next and that he didn't need to somehow work it out for himself.

The purpose of being in the room wasn't just to entertain Daniel with activities, but to get him involved in 2-way play, which is actually mutual communication with another person. The name that Mifne gives to this method of therapy that they have developed is *Reciprocal Play Therapy*. It is designed to create an environment where the therapist and the child are playing *together*. It would start by modelling an activity and inviting him to join in, and if that worked, to carefully watch what parts of it he enjoyed and expand those parts, bringing in as much reciprocal activity - such as turn-taking - as possible. Then we would "expand" it. Rather than doing one short activity and then moving directly on to something different when it was over - giving an impression of a haphazard succession of unrelated events - we were encouraged to take small activities that he liked, and naturally and spontaneously build on them to create more of a sense of coherent flow. This would facilitate more mutual play and more opportunity for intimacy to develop through it. So if, for example, we were going to use the toys blocks in the room to make a large bridge, we would show him what we were doing (by about half-way through our time there, his interest was easily aroused by such activity starting to take place near him), and try to get him involved, maybe showing him how to lay a brick and then encouraging him to lay one himself, leading to taking it in turns to lay bricks. That way we could really say that we built it together. Then, if he had shown interest, we might demonstrate walking over the bridge, and then invite him to do the same, taking it in turns to do that as well. In one session, we were taking it in turns to balance rubber rings on each other's heads, and this had run its course, so rather than switch to something else, we took those same rings that he had been enjoying and started doing other things with them. We ended up biting them (following his lead), balancing them on some toy animals, rolling them down the side of a broom to guide them to where we wanted them to go, then tossing them one after another across the floor - eventually trying to hit the previous one that had been tossed. It allowed Daniel to become more absorbed in the game and more conscious that he was playing it with another person. It led to his increasingly looking to that person as an integral part of the game and responding to them, meaning that reciprocity had been established and a greater degree of connection and intimacy was possible. Even tidying up after an activity could be expanded into something bigger. There was one session where the therapist was sweeping the floor after some messy play. She had a broom, and there was also a child's broom there that Daniel could use to join in if he wanted to. He picked it up and started copying her sweeping actions. It quickly turned into a short game of chase around the room with the brooms, which he enjoyed very much. After a while though, he became more absorbed in his own play with the broom and lost consciousness of the presence of the therapist, just sweeping along in his own thoughts. So in order to bring him back, the therapist made a little bridge out of a light mattress they'd been playing with, and put it as an obstacle in front of him, which he needed to climb through in order to move forwards. She turned this into a game where they took it in turns to go round and climb under the bridge, thus bringing him back into actively playing with her. It was about using an activity or interest that he evidently liked and developing it as a means of connecting with him, introducing as many reciprocal or communication elements into our play as we could. It was really giving him practice of life.

Of course, there were not always opportunities for such a natural expansion of the game to bring him back, and in such situations, we just went up to him, took him by the hand, and led him gently back to where we were going to sit so that we could continue what we were doing or introduce the next activity.

One thing that was noteworthy when watching the sessions through the glass was how much silence and stillness there was in them. This was to avoid filling the place with unnecessary sound and emotion, which would have been daunting for him. The sorts of sensory stimulation that are often used to appeal to children do not necessarily feel very enticing to autistic children, who experience them as an onslaught of chaos. Retaining calmness while remaining constantly open was key to making him feel safe and not at risk of an overwhelming flood of noise or excitement. There was, of course, a need for some talking: It was important to provide occasional commentary on what was happening, to give Daniel reassurance both in his understanding of what was going on, and in our confidence and conviction in what we were doing for him (thus containing him). Similarly, it was important to give him signposts as to what was about to happen next to help him avoid surprises (he would understand at least that *something* was going to happen, even if he didn't quite understand what), and to let him know why we might be doing something - for example, to explain that we were going to the adjoining room to get something and we would be back shortly, to avoid momentary confusion or disorientation about why he had been left alone. And it was of course necessary to keep affirming to him our pleasure to be there playing with him. But these verbal messages were kept brief and simple, so that he would be more likely to pick up bits of understanding from them, and also to avoid filling the intentionally calm space with additional sound. Our emotions, too, were kept low key for the same reasons. We expressed joy and sometimes even excitement, but without making theatrical displays of it, which would certainly have sent him back to interiorisation. And we learnt to read his responses to our communication, observing if there were any particular triggers for him to either engage more or disengage from us. For example he nearly always responded to peek-a-boo type games, and we often used these briefly to bring him back to a state of engagement, but he was nearly always pushed away by over-excitement on our part. It meant that, again, we needed to regulate our own emotions, and be alert not only to what was happening with Daniel, but also what was going on within ourselves and how that might be assimilated by him. We also learnt that he needed to be given his own time and space to absorb what was happening and to respond to it. Instead of getting worried when he didn't react at "normal" speed to an invitation or stimulus, we started to understand that he needed to be able to do so in his own time. At first, we had assumed that there was no interest because we got nothing back in what we considered to be a reasonable period of time. But we were encouraged to wait, and when we did, we found to our delight, that he was fully ready to participate, he just needed his processing time. So, often, we needed to slow ourselves down and ensure that he had really completed his interest in an activity before moving on to the next one.

Developing this ability to tune into him, and to find a way to show him that he was tuned into, was another really important component of his therapy. If we were going to encourage reciprocity in him, we needed to model it, and we needed to do that by being very cognisant of and very responsive to his changing condition. We received feedback at one point that it looked more as if we were performing for him than building a relationship with him. This was evident at moments when we were offering him activities and he wasn't responding at all. Rather than acknowledging his choice not to join in, we were carrying on speaking to him *as if* he was interested, oblivious to the reality that he had shown to us. Naturally, there was no way that closeness or intimacy could be built when we were unable to read our son, or acknowledge the message he was plainly giving us. We started to learn to notice, accept positively and respect with authenticity whatever he was expressing to us.

When he was frustrated by something, we responded to this by holding him so that he was comforted. When he was sad and cried, usually when Oksana or I left the room, he would be held, stroked and calmed as much as he needed. Even if he expressed anger, this did not evoke a challenging response from us – we accepted this too, though also would have had our limits if he had become violent. These limits would not have been expressed with a harsh voice or a wagging finger, but as a confident and loving reassurance that everything was going to fine, that he was big and strong enough to cope with whatever was happening, and that it was not okay to kick (or whatever he was doing); there were other ways to express himself, which we could help him to find. Sometimes a gentle, "there's no need to scream" was enough, as long as it was accompanied by a genuine acceptance of his condition at that moment. We learnt how important it was never to reject his distress or push it away because we didn't feel we knew how to cope with it – instead we had to increase our own confidence and capacity to cope.

The aim when comforting him, though, was not to give him unlimited soothing that would go on for ages. This would not have been a way to show him that he was capable of dealing with difficult situations himself. It was to give him the comfort he needed in order to feel able to cope again, and then to bring him back to managing himself independently. We might do this quite subtly. For example, if he was in distress and needed a cuddle, he might have a tendency to cling on to us for a long time. We would allow him to do this until he started to become more composed, but then, we might encourage him towards independence by, for example, sitting down and sitting him on our leg to speak to him. He would still be getting the closeness and reassurance along with our full attention, but his new physical position would encourage him to let go of the clinging, and would be a much better starting point for resuming our play on equal terms again. It was a way of containing him emotionally at the same time as promoting his resilience and confidence in his own capacity for independence.

The ability and confidence to contain Daniel made it possible to challenge him in areas where he may have had great reluctance to expand his horizons. This challenging had a clear purpose, which was to help him to understand that he didn't need to feel constrained by the limits he perceived in his abilities or tolerances. I am not using the word challenge to denote any sort of confrontation, rather a clear but gentle invitation to him to extend the range of possibilities available to him. One example was around his sensory issues. He had been very reluctant to touch any sort of grainy or moist materials, being repelled by their feel. While containing Daniel, it was possible to introduce some sensory experiences into his play without this seeming too threatening, and to make it feel safe to experiment. One therapist, who had been playing with a balloon with Daniel expanded that particular activity by taking out a can of shaving foam, and putting a dot of it on the balloon. Then he put his finger in it and put a blob of it on his nose. Daniel watched with some apprehension, and when he was offered the opportunity to copy this, he didn't totally recoil, and even very tentatively touched the foam with his finger. He pulled it back very quickly and wiped it ferociously on a towel, but with a little smile. Because of the calm and positive atmosphere that the therapist had created, this had not been a traumatic experience for Daniel, as it would otherwise have been. It was something that demonstrated to him his own capacity to cope with something he didn't think he would enjoy. He was in control, in the sense that he could break off from the activity at any time he wanted without any consequence and without fear of causing offence, and this gave him added reassurance that there was safety in this exploration. The therapists built on this a lot during our time there, and brought in increasing amounts of sensory play. Within a few days, he had used all sorts of materials that had previously been off limits, and had played, with ever-expanding tolerance, with foam, water (bathing dolls, etc), hand paints, sand and many more materials. He had also learnt to feel comfortable being caressed and massaged. We were advised to keep up this idea of continually challenging Daniel when we got back to England, to empower him to feel increasingly independent. We could also notice and challenge any habits of automatic or inward play, and even to take different routes when walking around town, so that he could learn to feel comfortable with things being done in a different way and could feel less fixed in about ways of doing things.

Essentially, Daniel had been continually challenged for the whole of his stay there – from having his pushchair taken away, to being separated from his parents, to being required to eat on our terms, to being assisted to recompose himself after moments of distress, to playing in different ways and with different sorts of materials. But this challenging had been done in such a respectful way that it turned out to be far less overwhelming for him in the long run than it would have been to allow things to continue in the way he had previously demanded. It was actually a very positive experience with a very positive outcome. When he finally got his pushchair back on the last day, he laughed excitedly at the prospect of getting into it again. But there was no longer any sign of the adamant dependence he had previously had on it. That, along with much else, had been broken, and there were no issues at all in handing it over to the cabin staff on the plane home.

So a tremendous amount happened during our time at the Mifne Centre in Israel. It truly was a turning point in our family's lives, and after a year of unrelenting misery, disappointment and pessimism, we were finally full of hope to a degree that we hadn't dreamed of, even when we had found out about the clinic.

We were going home with a totally different boy - more balanced, engaged, mature, self-regulating and happy than we could ever have imagined, and with the clear potential to keep on developing. And we had been given the tools to facilitate that onward development. But we were also alone now. We could call on support from Mifne via email or Skype whenever we needed it, but that was very different from actually being there and living the therapy with a clinic full of experts devoted to Daniel and our family. Our next challenge would be how to take what we had been given in Israel and successfully continue this work essentially on our owns.

Chapter 4 – What is Autism, Really?

I said in the introduction that I would be hard pressed to give more than a basic description of what autism actually is. That's not strictly true. I am not interested in getting into the intellectual debate about whether autism is a result of genetics or parenting or vaccines or environmental pollutants or a shock of some sort or a combination of some of these things or something else entirely. We could all add our thoughts to this discussion but we would just be guessing, and at the end of it all we still would not know, as the evidence is not there to definitively say which is correct. I'm not especially interested either in listing the set of attributes that are associated with the condition. This might be necessary and useful in identifying and diagnosing it, but doesn't give us much of an idea how to improve the lives of people who have it (teaching them social "rules" one by one - or worse, training them in these - is likely to be confusing and frustrating for them rather than meaningful or remotely fulfilling).   But from what we have learnt, particularly at Mifne, and from what we have observed first hand in our son, I do have a different sort of perspective on autism that I feel applies at least to our family's case, and I suspect to very many others.   I share it in the hope that it might transform how we see our autistic children, and by extension, how we behave towards them and what we can offer them.   The reflections in this chapter are purely personal.

Usually, when we think of autism, we do think about those common difficulties that autistic people seem to have, related to things such as social interaction and self-regulation.   But to me, these difficulties do not constitute autism.   These are not the characteristics of an autistic person.   Rather, they are the results of the coping strategies that autistic people feel compelled to use, which mask their true characteristics.   But why would they need a coping strategy?

It seems obvious to me that sensitivity is at the heart of autism.   Autistic people are extremely sensitive in many ways.   Sensory inputs that we might think of as unremarkable can be overwhelming to them.   Opening the curtains on a moderately sunny morning might feel like having a very bright flash light shone directly into their eyes at close range. A plate falling onto the kitchen floor might sound as disturbing as standing next to loud drilling on a building site without any earmuffs.

Along with this, there is emotional sensitivity. Somebody raising their voice a little while experiencing a twinge of impatience could feel like a devastating assault. In the years following Daniel's return from Israel, if we ever gently reprimanded him with very slightly raised voices, he would look as if he was being accused of murder. For months afterwards, he would be very wary of upsetting us, sometimes saying things like, "If I do that, Mama will be angry and the doors will shake." It is not only that the expression of the emotions was magnified for him, but it was as if he actually sensed and felt what we were feeling - unable to stop it entering him - even when we didn't express it outwardly. Perhaps this is one reason why autistic people often seem oblivious to what others are feeling - the magnitude of what it would take to cope with the common run of human emotions makes it too terrifying to even start to engage with them. It is precisely because they are so sensitive that they can only make a decision to cut themselves off from what is going on around them in order to protect themselves from the onslaught. It is a decision that costs them their true nature, but which they do not feel equipped to avoid, as the rest of us would not in a world that was just too much for *us*, whatever that would mean in each of our individual cases.

Another area of sensitivity is around things being "right" or "as they should be". This is often thought of as an area of inflexibility in autistic people, but what is at the root of it? Experts will tell us that it is a means of exerting control in a world in which they have little, as if that by itself gives us any meaningful insight into their experience or guidance on how to support them. I sense and believe that it comes from an inherent idealism they have that all people are well-intentioned, naturally inclined to be supportive, caring, trusting and ready to put the well-being of others above their own. Actually, I don't believe it is idealism for autistic people at all - for them it is just what they naturally expect because it is what they themselves are naturally ready to bring to this life. We could call it love. But what superhuman level of strength would it take to maintain this degree of love and openness while constantly witnessing and experiencing amplified malice, aggression and cold-heartedness all around, and being totally unable to comprehend how anyone could possibly be capable of such things? Every instance of it would shatter their loving hearts until it was no longer tolerable. I'm sure this is why autistic people close down, and then try to exercise this "control" over whatever they can, with so much else being unbearably wrong around them.

This loving nature in our son, which has found expression in recent years, was still there and deeply inherent within him during the darkest months of his autism. He was the same human being. He was simply too overwhelmed by his surroundings to be able to exhibit it. His sensitivity to his surroundings prevented him from fully engaging with them.

We often hear professionals talking of "*over*-sensitivity", but isn't this an undue judgement? A kitchen scale that measured to a hundredth of a gram couldn't be described as "over-sensitive". It has a sensitivity proportionate to the level of refinement required by the job it has to do. However, if a 5kg rock was dropped onto it, it would at best start to malfunction - giving unreliable or incomprehensible readings - and at worst be destroyed. If that same rock was dropped onto a set of industrial scales, it would have no noticeable impact on them whatsoever, and they would carry on working as normal. The kitchen scale, being so refined, can give a much better quality of reading than the industrial scales could ever do, but at the cost of its resilience. The analogy is obvious. Think what the growing community of autistic people could bring to this world, how they could improve it - in ways we could never imagine and could never hope to do ourselves - if only we let them; if only we recognised the richness and refinement within each of them that they came here so ready and willing to give; if only we didn't keep piling 5kg rocks on top of them.

When we look at it from this perspective, it is clear

that it is not the autistic person who has the problem, it is the rest of us. It is we who have permitted ourselves to routinely hurt each other in the course of expressing ourselves and of trying to get what we want. It is we who have cultivated a life of competition and of comparing ourselves to others in an attempt to bolster our own sense of self-worth. It is we who have come to value the possessions or status that we acquire more than we do the feelings of our fellow human beings. It is we who fuel a politics that is more of a tribal strategy sport between rival parties than it is about finding consensual ways to meet the needs of our people. It is we who seek titillation in the conflicts and torments of others, and who populate even our mainstream entertainment and news with voyeuristic tension, violence, cruelty and devastation. It is we who have allowed our senses and emotions to be relentlessly over-stimulated in pursuit of artificial excitement. In doing all of this we have created a world of sheer horror for our autistic children. Is it any wonder that these supremely sensitive beings are shocked into incapacity by their total immersion in such an intense environment from which they have no respite? Is it even possible to simultaneously possess both the angelic qualities that these people inherently have, and the thick skin that is required to survive here? The difference between "us" and "them" is that we have become complicit in this distortion of our human nature and hardened to it, while they, pure in heart as they are, are not able to even conceive of becoming so.

When the world hurts us, we externalise the pain, turning it into anger, hatred, resentment, revenge and recycling it back out to others, thus perpetuating a world of suffering; while they could never dream of doing such a destructive thing, and are unable to comprehend how anyone could. Instead, they can only internalise it, and are thus forced into an isolated inward retreat.

And we call autism a disability!

These children, who are so overwhelmed and cut off from this world, would thrive and prosper in a different world where people were primarily motivated by a warm sense of community and primarily focused on bringing positivity and support into each other's lives. I can imagine them being fully integrated and perfectly balanced in such a world. Many, who currently rock and fail to communicate, would be natural and pioneering leaders of absolute integrity, with a clear purpose to safeguard and enhance the well-being of others, as their true nature is able to freely assert itself. It would be a *safe place* for them to project themselves without fear of undue sensory stimulation or utterly poisoning emotional negativity; and would allow their as yet unseen but nevertheless exceptional qualities to shine through. Rather than force them into retreat from this world, which is after all their rightful home as much as it is ours, couldn't we just make it into such a safe place? It might sound like a naïve and clichéd Utopian fantasy, and yet it is the hidden and usually ignored craving that each of us carries silently within ourselves.

Let us do all we can to bring as much of this ideal as possible into our lives, at least for our children to benefit from.

Chapter 5 – Moving Forward

We returned home from our visit to Mifne with a very different family life to the one we had left less than a month earlier. But now we had to think about how we were going to sustain it. For the first 3 weeks of our new life, everything had been organised and led by a dedicated clinic full of outstanding professionals. Now it was just us, trying as best we could to keep up a 6 hour a day programme in Daniel's room at home, with me back at work and Oksana looking after the practicalities of daily life.

For that reason, Mifne had very strongly recommended that we take on a professional child psychotherapist to assist with it. The only problem was, we had been more than wiped out financially by our trip to Israel, and there were a lot of hours each day to fill. I could do an hour in the morning before going to work, then Oksana could do a stint, but then we would need a therapist every day, else we would be done in little over 2 hours. As we couldn't afford one, we thought that we were not going to be able to continue with it as prescribed. We toyed with the idea of splitting the day into two parts, doing perhaps 2 and a half hours in the morning, and the same in the evening, with me doing the final hour when I came home from work. It could probably have worked - just - but my finish time wasn't always predictable, and my energy levels on my return were far from guaranteed (therefore neither was the quality of my input), and if we did that, there would have been no family time, which was also a critically important component of the programme, as he would have had to go to bed straight afterwards.

Fortunately, there was a student of biodynamic therapy in London at the time called Yael, who was from Israel and had had an association with the Mifne Centre when she'd been there. She had even worked to support another family in London who had visited the clinic. She very generously charged us her student rate rather than her professional one, which made it possible for us to go ahead (we were still going further into debt each month, but by amount that wasn't prohibitive). She joined us very soon after we returned, and made a wonderful connection with Daniel - she was a very important part of his life for nearly 3 years, and made a very warm and natural connection with him. She was invaluable to us throughout this period - and able to make sense of situations and phases that Daniel was going through which we wouldn't have understood by ourselves. This was especially true in the initial period, when we were starting our own home treatment. We are sure that she made a very big contribution to his continued progress, and still now he remembers her fondly and talks about her as one of his best friends. She initially came to us 3-4 times a week (which later went down to twice and then once as the hours in the room gradually reduced), and we looked to find a nursery that Daniel could go to for the other 2 days. He would have reduced hours in the room on those days.

We had been strongly advised in Israel to put Daniel in a nursery part time to accelerate his ability to feel comfortable around other children. The therapy in Israel, that we were about to continue in his room had been about being in a quiet place with a single adult. It was a carefully managed environment, and a very controlled one. However, the aim of it had been to begin to evoke capabilities in him that would enable him eventually to be able to manage, initially with support, in a regular environment, and it was thought that the earlier some element of this could be introduced, the better. This would be in small doses that would be more than balanced by large amounts of time in the room. He was to go for just 2-3 hours a day, twice a week, to begin with, and would have a one-to-one Key Worker who would be there to support him at all times. Once we engaged with the nursery, they helped to arrange the funding for this, which was not difficult as Daniel's needs were already clear and understood by the authorities.

We took a lot of care selecting a nursery, and we think now that we took too much care. We researched all nurseries in quite a large area around our home. Eventually we narrowed it down to ones that had an Ofsted "Outstanding" rating, though this seems to be quite a large proportion of nurseries (as opposed to schools, as we discovered a couple of years later), and looked more seriously at ones that mentioned their experience of looking after and integrating children with special needs. We had decided, after seeing how much potential there was in Daniel to evolve, that we didn't want to send him to a special nursery, or later to a special school, where there would be less opportunity to put that evolution into practice and to take it further to a gradual integration into regular life. However, along with that decision, we needed to accept as a consequence that the staff would not be experts in his condition or know how to manage him in an ideal way. They would be nursery nurses who would do their best, but who may not always fully appreciate what Daniel's needs were. That was difficult for us to come to terms with - especially after the attention to every detail of his and our own behaviour that we had been encouraged to pay during our treatment in Israel. There was no perfect solution, but on balance, a regular nursery was the only one that made sense in our circumstances.

After visiting many nurseries, we settled on one that was quite far away - it took nearly an hour to get there, using 2 busses each way. There were 2 Key Workers who shared responsibility for Daniel. They were very warm to him and he became very fond of one of them in particular. However, through no fault of their own, they were not always aware of how best to support him. We had some meetings with them before he started there, which helped a lot, and Yael visited them once he had started and observed him there and gave them support in how to deal with Daniel, which became ongoing on a very occasional basis. However, there was, naturally, a lot we could not see about what was going on there. This is normal, but we were especially keen to find out more, because of our concern about maintaining Daniel's progress and avoiding anything that might jeopardise it, which sometimes made us a little anxious, especially when Daniel seemed to have been thrown off balance during a day there. We were always positive with them and always asked them for details of what was happening in a collaborative and constructive way, but they would have picked up on some anxiety in us and therefore seemed to interpret our questions as an expression of disapproval in how they had been managing him. This was very far from the case, but after having learnt very effectively how to contain Daniel, we had not thought much about how to contain the staff in the nursery (and I think later in his initial months at school as well), by making more of an effort to remind *ourselves* that everything was going to be fine with Daniel, and being very calm and open with the staff about why we were asking. We should also have given them more genuine praise for what we appreciated in what they were doing, and ultimately had more trust in Daniel's resilience. They may still - without much experience of the condition - not have understood why we wanted to know so much more than other parents did, and they might still have put us down as over-anxious parents, but they may have felt less uncomfortable, or even intimidated, by our approaches.

The distance was also problematic. It was nice for Daniel to have the routine, and he enjoyed his journeys on the bus, especially after the first few weeks, but it was exhausting for us, and over time used up a lot of energy that might otherwise have been more usefully deployed in other ways. I took him there before work when I was able, but on days when I wasn't, Oksana needed to take him herself, and in doing so, lost the potential for a whole morning of getting things done, as it wasn't really worth coming back home only to leave again very shortly afterwards. We hadn't really been very sensible choosing a nursery so far away, and after a few months, switched to another nursery, which proved to be at least as good, just a very few minutes' walk away from our home. This simplified life greatly.

Setting up his room for the ongoing therapy, we

made it as much like the room at Mifne as possible. He already slept on duvets on the floor, so it was easy to move them away in the morning to make a spacious play room with not much in it, and to bring them back in when he wanted to sleep. We put a shelf high up on the wall and filled it with boxes of play materials, toys, toy animals, games and so on. We installed a large mirror across the back wall, as we had had in the therapy room in Israel, and which had not only made the room feel bigger, but had also expanded his opportunities for play and even contact (he loved watching himself in it and had often felt safer making eye contact with others through the mirror than directly). We installed a surveillance camera in the room, so that we could watch each other during the sessions on the computer downstairs, and also record the sessions to watch them later and learn from them (in practice we rarely had time for this, but it was beneficial when we did). Basically, we resumed the therapy with the 2 of us and Yael, as much as possible in the same vein as we had done it in Israel. We checked in regularly to give each other feedback and to review what was changing in Daniel and what in turn needed to change in our behaviour in the room. This kept us sharp and helped to avoid our falling into a lazy routine in the room that would not have served him. We filled in a report together every fortnight and sent it to the Mifne Centre, who gave us feedback on what was going on and gave us direction, as well as helping us to fine-tune what we were doing. Within a few weeks, we recruited two more child psychotherapy students with an interest in autism. We had found them by approaching the Colleges in London with relevant courses, and they came to participate with us as volunteers to support their own learning as well as to help Daniel. For a while, our house became a vibrant hub of professional treatment, at least for a couple of days a week when everyone was there. And importantly, Daniel felt comfortable with it because it was familiar and continued to be fun for him.

Within a few weeks, though, all of us began to feel that we had run out of ideas for things to do in the room. However many possibilities there were, they did get used up very quickly when he was in there for 6 hours most days. Mifne gave us advice, reminding us of some fallback ideas, but in all honesty, I think we all felt a little stale for a while, especially myself and Oksana, as we didn't want the sessions to get repetitive. He even seemed to be outgrowing some of the sorts of activities we had done in Israel. We needed new ideas. We needn't have been too worried about this (though that's easy to say now). The key thing was spending quality time with him in a quiet environment and encouraging mutual play. Often we wouldn't even need to use the ideas we had prepared during a session in the room, as we would have increasing amounts of natural and spontaneous communication with him. While we did a lot of the more structured activities like drawing, painting, playing with materials, and so on, often, the most fun we had, and the most reciprocal participation, was with impromptu play that happened without any preparation, such as making stories with his toy animals that he was invited to join in, or drawing together on the mirror, or bouncing on a big pre-natal ball that we still had and that we used a lot in the room, or just exchanging looks or sounds, or singing him nursery rhymes and getting him to join in the actions. He responded very happily to all such things. And there were so many ways to use the play materials that we had in there. There were little star stickers as just one example, and just sticking them on paper was great fun for him. Of course, we had to be careful that it didn't become a game that he played repetitively by himself without consciousness or consideration for the person with him, so we might make sure we took it in turns to choose and stick stickers, and made sure he understood that this was how it was to work. This kept him aware of our presence and engaged with us. Then we might expand it by drawing a line between 2 stars that we had stuck down. Or they could be stuck on balloons, which might then be blown up, and it was interesting to learn about what would happen to the stickers when they were. We might then play a game of bouncing the balloon to each other - then help his toy animals to do the same, and when the balloon play had run its course, we might challenge him a little by preparing him for the fact that we were going to burst the balloon. Other times, we might use the chairs, the ball and the little table in the room as the base of a climbing frame and slide that we would make with planks of wood that we kept in the room. We might build these up and then help him to climb up and balance as he walked across the frame towards the slide that he slid down. None of this involved mind-blowingly original play concepts. It was very simple and spontaneous play, but play that Daniel would never have understood or shown any interest in before our treatment. And it was the safe environment of the room, of which our own inviting and containing presence was a critical part, that enabled this incredible expansion of his ability to interact with us all. Nevertheless, despite the success of treating Daniel in the room, which went on for around 2 years (with reducing hours , before phasing it out altogether in the third year), we remember that our period of doing so was partly characterised for us by a constant feeling of inadequacy in terms of keeping ideas fresh and dynamic. We needed to continually work to overcome this feeling to avoid it being unconsciously transferred to him in how we played.

While continuing to use the room to support this expansion in Daniel's interactive abilities, we also wanted to very gradually start to enable him to bring this new openness into the world. He was happy to do so, but it was not easy at first. Going to the nursery was the first critical step, and in his early weeks, it seems that he needed to be either constantly attended to by his Key Worker, or left alone to explore the toys in there, oblivious to the other children. We had chosen a relatively quiet nursery, but even so, the amount of noise in the environment was a shock for him and prevented him from being able to relax and open up further for a while. Even at this early stage, though, it gave him the ability to be around other children in a busy environment without being completely overwhelmed by their presence. He also learnt to feel more comfortable there and was able to let himself start to enjoy himself in spite of any environmental challenges. He seemed particularly happy when it was Circle Time and the children were read to or sang songs together.

Even the journey to the nursery was a sort of training, and it seemed overwhelming to him at first. While he was by this time mostly open and happy at home, as soon as we started walking in the street, he became very withdrawn, looking down uncommunicative and appearing not to hear us when we spoke. It must have been the busyness and the sounds of the road, and the other people. It just seemed too much for him in the early weeks, but he did gradually become accustomed to it, and we were happy to notice that within a few months, he was very comfortable walking down a street and communicating with us at the same time. Of course, we never pushed him in any of this, and let him go at his own pace, respecting his limits at all times, and helping him to understand that everything was fine as much as we could.

We also, very occasionally, introduced another child into the therapy room. These were children of around his age whose parents were happy for them to participate in our programme, and at first, these sessions were always led by Yael, as they were much less straightforward than the other ones. Both children required a lot of facilitation. It would have been easy for one of them to have felt as if they weren't getting enough attention, or for each of them to end up playing on their own as if the other wasn't there, when the purpose of the session was to help Daniel to become aware of the other child and to start to feel comfortable interacting with them. The first girl who came to join was someone who Daniel was already fond of, and the first thing that happened each time she came to the room was that he became very excited and unable to regulate himself. He seemed incapable of staying still, and could only run around laughing excitedly. Yael (and later we) offered very calm support and acted as a model of composure and serenity to help calm him as best she could, though in the early instances of this, his excitement continued for hours after the session. It was similar when we went to visit my family in Wolverhampton. Daniel liked his cousins very much, but the first few times they were together after we returned from Israel, he completely lost his balance, becoming seriously over-excited. All we could do was to act, again, as a model of calm and composure around him. Eventually this phase passed, and he learnt to better manage himself in such situations, just as he had previously learnt to function in the face of the hustle and bustle in the street.

At times, he showed great warmth to people we met, even on the bus, who we had never met before. That was a phase that passed, but he did develop more affection for people in our lives. In other situations though, such as in his nursery, he seemed not to understand that other children were actual people with their own feelings. Sometimes he might play with them as if they were props or toys (for example landing toy aeroplanes on their heads), other times, he might even push them if he wanted to get somewhere and they were in the way. It was never done with anger or malice, just a lack of understanding that they were capable of being annoyed or hurt. This was a short phase, but awareness and understanding of others, especially other children has always, has always been and remains the area where he needs most support. 18 months or so after we returned home, as he was approaching 4, a paediatric assessment placed him close to age-appropriate levels in all areas of his development (according to the categories they assessed) apart from Social Understanding, where he remained significantly behind. In order to address this further, we have more recently started working with the Davis Method, which is described in chapter 6.

One of the ways in which we were advised to help him process and better understand social issues was through Symbolic Play.   This was using his toy animals or (preferably) people figures to enact, as part of regular play, the sorts of situations that he might be finding difficult, so that he could understand the impact of one person's actions on other people without being challenged directly about his own behaviour.   That would only have baffled and unsettled him.   Without the intuitive understanding of consequence, which he hadn't yet developed, any attempt to tell him how to or not to behave would make the social world into even more of a confusing and impenetrable minefield.   Symbolic play was a natural, non-threatening and fun way to start to introduce an appreciation of other people as beings with the same, but distinct, needs and wants as he had.   It was an excellent foundation for the deepening of this exploration that started to take place a couple of years later when we began using the Davis Method.

So if, for example, Daniel had pushed another child at nursery, we might play a game during which it just so happens that one of his toys pushes another because they are in the way.   Daniel is very interested in scenarios we enact with his toys and is usually quite disturbed when observing any conflict or distress, so when something like this happened, he would try to intervene to protect the toy that was being pushed.   We could then ask him why he was intervening and what it was that made him concerned about that situation.   He would most likely say that he didn't want the second toy to be hurt. Then we could work out together what happened and what the toy that pushed might not have understood, and how they could have handled it better, in a way that respected the other toy. We could arrive together at a general understanding that pushing or similar behaviour is not what we want to be doing because we don't want to hurt someone else. Thus, through play, we could completely examine what had happened in the nursery and take lessons from it, with no reference to it whatsoever. He may well not have been able to handle a direct conversation about it. Similarly, when he went through a phase of having his own ideas about how to play and getting very stressed if any other child had any intentions that might impinge on them, we made a scenario where 2 of his favourite animals – who were best friends with each other – wanted to play together but had different ideas about what to do, and started arguing. Again, disturbed by the conflict and wanting to help his animals to remain happy, Daniel stepped in and proactively mediated between them, asking what they both wanted to do and suggesting they play one game first and then the other. Needless to say, the animals implemented this and were very happy with it. We were able to arrive at a general understanding that if people have different ideas about how to play, they could take turns to play each other's preferred game, or one of them could even be flexible and just play the other person's game – it was still a game where they could both have fun. Most importantly, we observed that whatever the situation, there were no grounds for stress as it could easily be resolved. Again, Daniel got a full understanding – which had actually come purely from him – about the situation that he had been finding difficult, without needing to discuss it directly. Otherwise he might have felt very uncomfortable, as if he was being reprimanded for something he didn't really comprehend. We are sure that symbolic play greatly accelerated his learning of many basic social lessons, and we also used it more generally to learn about sharing and being flexible.

This became possible to do much more effectively once language started to come, which actually happened very quickly. Mifne had told us that we should expect him to start speaking about 6 months after we returned. In the event, within a couple of months, he was already at least back to the level of speech he had been at before his regression began. Within 3 or 4 months, he had a growing vocabulary. At first, he only said the first syllable of each word to convey its meaning, but he was soon speaking in full words, then short sentences, then full sentences. It was as if he was making up for lost development time with a phase of expedited language learning. And with the ability to speak came a whole new phase of development. Our work in the room changed a lot as we used language to communicate much more, though we still had to be careful to keep it as sparse and simple as possible to avoid a retreat into an intellectual, rather than experiential, understanding of the world. We needed to work to keep the intimacy of a much less verbal connection alive after language entered the picture. He was already understanding a lot of what we said – much more than we had realised - and he was now, with his new language capabilities, letting us know it more of the time. I remember a couple of times talking to Oksana about various things, while Daniel was playing quietly with his toys, and his absorbing more than we imagined. Once, it was about how I needed to change my job, and he unexpectedly came in decisively with, "I will help you find one!" Another time, I was telling her about a dream I had had where someone had taken my phone, and he suddenly started to cry. We thought he might have hurt himself with something he was playing with so we asked him what had happened, and sobbing, with tears running down his face, he exclaimed, "I don't want them to take Daddy's phone." It was touching to see the caring part of him becoming more and more apparent as his language developed. He routinely wanted to look after us if there was a hint of anything being wrong. Even when I was pretending to be scared to go on the Pirate Ship at Legoland, he assured me, "Don't worry, I will hold your hand." It reminded us of the beginnings of the emergence of such qualities when he was a baby, just before his regression began, and we remembered one time from back then when Oksana had been giving me a massage because my back hurt, and when I groaned, he must have thought I was being cruelly subjected to pain, so he pulled himself up in panic and tried to push Oksana away from me. Now we were seeing the resurgence of this character trait, and it was not just with us – he often became very affected and concerned if he saw anybody undergoing any sort of unpleasantness. Other children of his age might have ignored such things or laughed, or in some cases even inflicted misery of each other, but Daniel has always seemed to feel the pain of the other person as his own.

The degree to which he was sensitive to others' misery and sadness was awe-inspiring, but left unregulated, it would inevitably prevent him from fully participating in normal life. Even if we were just pretending to be sad for a moment, he would start to cry. If he was already crying and he caught a glimpse of himself crying in the mirror, the vision of sadness that he saw would send him into more intense crying. It was so acute that if we were reading a book to him and one of the pictures in it had somebody looking sad, or in danger, or if anything was happening that might make them sad, we wouldn't be able to go on reading it. Once, we bought him a book that told a lovely story where a cat and a dog lived together and one day the dog was hungry and ate the cat's food while she was away. The book went on to describe how the cat got angry with the dog and threw him out, and he eventually learnt to respect the cats things, and they lived together again very happily. But we never got that far, because as soon as

Daniel understood that the dog had eaten the cat's food, and the cat would come home to an empty dish, he screamed "no!" and slammed the book shut. It was so painful for him that we couldn't persuade him to look at it for several weeks, and then only with adequate preparation about what would happen in the story and very much reassurance that they would both be happy in the end. Even then, as we read it, he anxiously covered any pictures of sad or angry faces with his hands (he still does this when he sees something disturbing in a book) If a scary sound or a hint of anything potentially sad came on the computer, he would go and hide behind the curtain until it was over. It was hard to know how to manage this and use it to strengthen him, without it coming across as trying to push him into feeling okay (or pretending to feel okay) with something that was clearly not okay for him. The best we could do was to keep containing him – in such cases being models of people who can show compassion and understanding in a balanced way without being destabilised by the things we were seeing. That way, we were not only reassuring him that we (who he trusted) did not feel there was anything to be worried about; we were also giving him the understanding that actually it's fine to feel sad about things, but it is very useful as well to keep the broader perspective that ultimately everything is okay. Later, whenever we got emotional about anything, he began to reassure *us* that everything was okay, which showed excellent learning on his part and it was wonderful to see him channelling his concern in an obviously helpful way (though it was also a reminder to us that we weren't being especially good models in those moments). Still now, he suffers when he observes sadness in other people, and is keen to help them if at all he can. We respect and admire this trait in him.

It coincided with a period when he was becoming generally more settled and interactive, at least with those adults who were close to him. He started coming of his own accord to show us and share with us things that he may have drawn or made. Previously we had doubted whether this would ever happen. Even more joyful for us was when he started to show demonstrable affection to us, clearly happy to see us and be with us. He even exclaimed verbally many times how he liked us, though it was his beaming smile and unfiltered enthusiasm that testified to this more than the words. Sometimes his appreciation was not expressed until later. Once he seemed to be absorbed in his own play with 2 toy cars and I asked him whether I could join him. He passed one of the cars to me - a yellow one - without looking at me, and told me it should follow his red car. I did as he asked, but he didn't seem to offer me any more of a role in this game, and it finished soon afterwards. Later in the day, he came to me and looked at me with deep gratitude and said, "you played with me with the yellow car!" He also became gradually better at regulating himself, and even his nursery noticed that it was no longer like the end of the world for him if things didn't go as he wanted them to. And he became more independent in terms of his self-care, migrating easily from the potty to the toilet; and his transition from nappies was very smooth.

His language development brought more opportunities for him to explore and try to understand life, or just to have fun with it. Soon after learning to speak in nouns with a good vocabulary, he started to experiment with saying the opposite of what he could see, for humorous effect. For example, 2 of his favourite toys at that time were called Tiger and Cheetah, and he enjoyed telling us the Tiger was Cheetah, and Cheetah was Tiger, with a mischievous smile. One morning, Oksana had said that she could see a spoon under the table, and Daniel, quite rightly, said, "No, spoon *by* table, not under table." The next day he came into the lounge waving a shoe horn around and said, "Shoe horn under table." We told him that he was holding the shoe horn, and he grinned widely, and said, "I said shoe horn under table. I make mistake, like Mama." Other times, when he learnt a new word, such as "horrible", he would say, with a cheeky and delighted grin, things like "Mama horrible, Daddy horrible. You [meaning himself] nice."

He referred to himself as "you" for a long time. We assumed that this was because we addressed him as you so often that he didn't realise that the word "I" is used to speak about oneself. But it was explained to us by the therapists at Mifne, and it was supported by what we later learnt when we started with the Davis Method, that this confusion of pronouns was not a linguistic issue, but revealed a real confusion in his mind about his own separateness from other people. We were advised not to correct him, but instead to give him a clear model of speaking about ourselves and other people, even indicating decisively with hand gestures who we were talking about. We did this, and after several months, he began naturally to use the pronouns correctly.

There were other ways that he used language to make sense of things or to process things he found difficult. It was revealing to see how profoundly he could be affected by what we might consider to be the most inconsequential things. Once, he heard a car outside and exclaimed, "big blue car!" having decided that that's what it was. So we opened the window to look at it, and it turned out to be a small green car. And that, we thought, was the end of that situation. But for many days after this, Daniel regularly turned very serious and said, "Not big blue car. Small green car. Bye, bye, big blue car." Another time, in an episode of what was (and still is) his favourite cartoon, Postman Pat, there was a moment when Pat had a fall and needed to be helped by a doctor. There was nothing remarkable about it - it wasn't a particularly shocking or traumatic fall - but again it led to several days of his repeating, "Pat fall down. Doctor help Pat. Pat happy." It was as close as he ever came to obsessive repetition of language - we think we managed to avoid more of it by the work we did during and after Mifne to keep things fresh, find new ways of doing and expressing things and challenge any repetitive tendency. But we were more concerned about how he could have been so deeply impressed by such little things. We were sure it wasn't new, and it was just that he was now able to think these things out loud. We were advised to help him process these anxieties by speaking with him openly in a natural, supportive and non-repetitive way about them and exploring with him what actually happened; and to avoid simply agreeing with him (and definitely to avoid becoming impatient with the repetition).

The way he used language also indicated an attempt to rationalise what he must have experienced as chaos all around. He seemed to be justifying his likes and dislikes with spurious generalised rules. For example, when he wanted to express that he didn't want to wear some particular clothes, he would say, "no, these are dry." Or if he didn't want to eat something or read something, he would say, "no, this is too big," as if that explanation added credibility to his preference. It must have reflected, on some level, his perception of how people reason and make decisions - he must have seen it as a nonsensical but necessary aspect of communication that he needed to try to emulate. We tried to support him in understanding how better to use reasoning through symbolic play. For example, on one occasion, I was playing with him with his soft animals and had them each give different reasons why they couldn't go into a small space. A toy dog said, "I can't go into that box because I'm brown." Daniel found this hilarious, and immediately corrected the dog, saying, "No! You can't go in there because you're too big." It was a way of getting him to understand how to use reason correctly, while having fun and without drawing attention to anything needing to be corrected. So this improved quickly, but the tendency to create general rules to justify his preferences remained for some time more. There was once that I mistakenly put my toothpaste on his brush and when we started to clean his teeth, he briefly cried. I realised what I'd done, and said, "Sorry, Daniel, I used my toothpaste instead of yours. It's very strong isn't it?" and he immediately turned this into an elaborate rule that should always apply in all circumstances, saying, "Boys shouldn't use this toothpaste because it is very strong and boys don't like strong toothpaste. This toothpaste is too strong for boys, that's why I don't like it." Even when there was no problem, he would do the same. Once, when he was clearly tired, I told him that if he had a good sleep, this would make him feel better, and within a second, he generalised this into, "If boys sleep for a long time, they will feel better in the morning." It was as if he felt the need to provide a universal intellectual explanation of his preferences, not out of a need to justify them, but as a means of making sense of them and of their place in the world.   For a child with autism who has a strong mind and who is still uncertain about how things work and what their own place is, the temptation to retreat into the intellect to find reassurance and apparent coherence must be very alluring, but we didn't want this to become established as his way of managing his uncertainties.   We were encouraged to start to model expressing our own wants and needs in a more explicit way and without justifications, and gradually, he became less dependent on concocting generalised logical explanations in support of his own wishes, and became more trustful of simply expressing them.

In a similar way, he used language as a tool to console himself when things were not as he wished.   If something wasn't as he wanted it to be, he changed the language that he applied to it to make it more acceptable. For example, he went through a phase of demanding a whole piece of kitchen paper (which he called "big paper") every time he wanted to wipe his nose.   We didn't let him have one, and insisted on his using a piece of toilet paper instead ("small paper").   On one occasion, after a session of crying in protest, he took the toilet paper and showed us that it was okay because, "this little-bit-big paper."   It was actually a creative means of coming to terms with what we required of him while still feeling okay about it because he was actually getting part of what he had asked for, according to his new description. Similarly, he knew that engines were in the front of cars, but when we saw a picture of a racing car and told him that the engine was in the back of that car, he was quite distressed and told us through tears that we were wrong and that the engine was in the front. We did our best to contain him, remaining very calm and showing him that we understood his distress, and at the same time reassuring him that it was okay that this car had an engine in the back, as not all cars are the same. The next morning, when we came downstairs, he went straight back to that picture and said, "Engine in back - I no like that idea. 2 engines in car!". We were so impressed with his willingness to come to terms with this new idea and at least partially accept what we had explained to him that it didn't seem appropriate or even necessary to point out to him at that point that it isn't really possible to come to a compromise on facts. Another time, when he lost his hat in the park and it distressed him very much, he eventually assuaged his distress with the idea that "Thomas [his favourite cartoon train at the time] will find my hat." He didn't have any real expectation of getting the hat back, but was actually happy to leave the park once he had had this idea. We neither corrected him, nor joined him in believing this, but, as we had been advised to do in such situations, we congratulated him on his being a big boy and accepting what had happened. Slowly, over time, he has become more able to cope with such losses without reverting to fantasy.

In relation to the development of language, as well as much else, I must pay special tribute to Oksana, who found it within herself to willingly make special sacrifices again and again.   Before going to Mifne, we had spoken at home both in English and in her native Russian.   Between us, we alternated every few days, and to Daniel, we spoke in our own language to him most of the time; myself in English, Oksana in Russian.   But because of the lack of language development, we were stongly advised by Mifne to speak only one language at home until he was 7, in order to give him the chance to attune to that language and grow into it.   Oksana was devastated by this, and it prompted many tears from her.   She understood the importance of doing so and readily agreed to it, but also knew that in one stroke she was limiting her ability to communicate freely with him (she still didn't feel able to fully express herself in English at that time), and probably losing her dream of Daniel growing up to be bilingual.   She "negotiated" a final few days of speaking Russian to him, and the retention of a few choice words, and has since been steadfast in talking with him in English.   Only now that he is 6, we are teaching him a few basic words of Russian.

With food, the situation was similar.   Like many mothers, she was very anxious about her son getting enough to eat on a regular basis, which was compounded by her own anxieties around food that she had inherited from her past. As we implemented the approach to food that Mifne had recommended to us - of making him responsible for his food intake and being especially careful not to bring any of our emotions or worries around food into the picture - she was forced to make fundamental inner-shifts in her attitude to his eating, and to become able to be genuinely calm and trusting during periods when Daniel hardly ate for several meals at a time (it had to be genuine, as he would have detected any unexpressed anxiety, which would have undermined the strategy and increased rather than decreased his food issues). The approach was successful, but was a colossal stretch for Oksana, which was further compounded when we tried a very restricted diet for Daniel for several months (more details in the next chapter) in the hope of alleviating some of his difficulties.

There were further compromises Oksana needed to make around the messy play that we had been encouraged to offer as a way of gently expanding Daniel's tolerance of different materials that he had been averse to. She has always been very concerned to keep the house in as close to a perfect condition as possible, and inclined to avoid anything that could compromise this wherever possible. Now, it was she who was being asked not only to pro-actively offer activities with water, clay, sand and paint, which could easily cause the house to look constantly suboptimal, but even to do so in a way that assured Daniel that this was something to be comfortable with. It entailed making further major adjustments within herself, which she did without complaint.

There were many further areas of sacrifice that she made, but these were the most notable ones. There was also a lot that she personally contributed to Daniel's recovery that yielded wonderful results which may well not have taken place without her. During this period, Daniel was becoming more demonstrably affectionate towards us, asking for hugs and saying very warm loving things to us. We are sure that this is because Oksana had always persisting in offering him continual love and affection herself, whatever the response or lack of response. Even in the days of his deepest regression, she had never stopped sitting next to him for long periods, gently stroking him and just being there with him and for him. And as his communicative tendency re-emerged, she embellished her presence with a very natural and creative ability to play with him. I was surprised by the ease at which she connected with him and offered him many very imaginative ideas for activities, which surely increased his inclination to participate in life.

So these 2 years of initially very intense and then gradually reducing therapy after our return from Israel saw a lot of progress. Daniel had become more settled, more happy, able to express himself verbally and to regulate himself when things went wrong, and he became more able to interact meaningfully with us as well, showing us genuine affection on a regular and increasing basis. His play had also become much more creative and less repetitive or classically autistic. While he still enjoyed putting his animals in a line, he did it now with more of a purpose or a story to it, and became increasingly open to arranging them in different ways, like in a circle so that they could see each other, or even in small groups so that they could talk or play together. He became spontaneously very creative. I remember one time when he was playing with cars with some toy people in them. The cars were going round and round in some sand, but rather than that being the entirety of the game, as it might have been a few weeks earlier, he had the cars stop on each circuit to deal with an imaginary problem, and it was a different problem each time - it might have been ice on the floor, or a hole in the sand, or someone falling out of the window and they had to stop to bring him back. It was new, and it showed that he was absorbing the flexibility that we were trying to impart to him, and embracing it. I learnt that he responded very well to that sort of creativity on our part as well. He took great delight when I intervened in a traffic jam scenario that he had created shortly after that, when I kept finding new reasons why the driver of the lorry at the front wouldn't move even though the cars behind were beeping their horns at him. First, it was because he was in a deep sleep, then, when he woke up he needed to tidy his lorry, then he was thirsty so he left his van to go to a café (which Daniel immediately created from blocks for him and proudly gave the name, "The Bake-Nut Café"), and when he returned, he felt sleepy again and needed another rest, and so on. Daniel became more excited and involved with each new explanation, and with the continued beeping of the cars behind. It showed how he was learning both to share his play and to explore and participate in new and surprising ideas rather than simply fall back on the same unvaried routines of play. It was a sign of real progress.

But it wouldn't be truly representative of this period to say that it was an undeviating upward curve. There were times of real concern about apparent regression during these months. At one point it looked like he was going back to his distant or repetitive habits like spinning or staring into space or looking lost or lining up his toys in a straight line. Other times he went through periods of being very unsettled and easily upset and unable to cope, or where his tendency towards apparently random sensitivities returned, such as a fear of water near his face. These phases lasted for shorter or longer periods, but they always passed. Sometimes, we could understand what had triggered them. The fear of water on his face, for example, had originated when we had needed to put some drops in his eyes, which he had hated.   Other times, we understood the origin much later .   For example, there was a time in late 2013 where he suddenly developed a severe and worrying stutter, as well as becoming generally more withdrawn and disoriented and developing a habit of humming.   This lasted for a very long time and we were very concerned that all his progress was being wiped out. It slowly waned over a period of months, and we eventually traced it back and understood that it had started the day after an early visit to the school that he would be going to the following year for what we thought would be a light and informal introduction to the place and some of the staff.   An outgoing senior member of staff decided that it would be a good idea for Daniel to join the in with the activities of the Reception class.   We expressed our reservations that this might be too much for him, but we were confidently reassured that in all of her experience this was best practice and an excellent way to bring the best out in the child, and anyway, he would have someone sitting next to him to help him.   Reluctantly, and against our better judgement, we agreed, but were horrified to see that the children were being asked, at a rapid pace, to reproduce letters that they had learnt (which Daniel hadn't, of course) on little blackboards that were handed out.   He was clearly overwhelmed by this sudden and bewildering expectation of him, and by the time he had taken a blackboard and vaguely understood that he had to do something with it (he had no idea what), they were all swiftly collected back again, leaving him feeling lost and confused. It had clearly had a more profound effect than we had realised.

But often, there was no way to understand what had triggered these difficult phases at all. They may have been induced by tiny events that had passed us by unnoticed but which had affected Daniel much more than we could have known. The fact that they arose at all demonstrated his level of sensitivity, that we always needed, and still need, to be mindful of. But the fact that they passed, often quite quickly, testified to his resilience, which it was easy to forget about when they were occurring. We were advised by Mifne to try to minimise their occurrence and severity by giving him adequate preparation of any expected change or potentially difficult event, and if possible, to make it into something positive and even exciting. We were also advised to try again to find a child psychotherapist for him to help him process any issues of underlying anxiety which may have been making him susceptible to these phases, but the biggest difficulty we had was finding one locally why we felt comfortable with. We searched and searched and spoke to many psychotherapists, but the enormous majority of them, to our minds, sounded detached, aloof, clinical and academic in their approach, which made us apprehensive and which contrasted starkly with the experience we had had in Israel, where the team of psychotherapists who had treated us had been very much guided by their hearts in building a relationship with Daniel and all of us. They had always been clear where the final responsibility lay for the improvement of our situation (with us, of course), but they were not overly adamant or self-protective about this, and allowed lines to be briefly crossed when that would allow for significant progress to be made. They did not appear to feel the need to adamantly retain a strict distance in order to ensure they didn't get "involved" or to protect themselves from feeling exposed, and this was of great benefit to the treatment.

Eventually, we did come across someone who we felt might be suitable to work with Daniel and we went to her for a while, but a few months after we began, she went on maternity leave, and so that wasn't able to continue. We never did find another.

When Daniel was 4 in 2013, sessions in the room were reducing to 2 shorter days per week, and a couple of hours on 4 more days to help him process and recover from the day's events. The balance of his life had shifted from spending most of the time in therapy in his room with occasional excursions into the world, to spending the majority of his time in the world, with regular and much shorter sessions in the room to give him additional support. Sessions were to reduce further over the coming months until they were phased out altogether. As part of that process, we began to leave the room for some parts of the sessions and apply the same principles of reciprocal communication in more authentic activities, like cooking something together or laying the table or even just playing hide and seek around the whole house or building a train track in the lounge. We could look back and be very grateful for the previous 2 years of improvement.

But while very positive, they had been an exhausting time for us. Creating and managing such an intense programme of so many hours over such a long period, as well as leading a busy life had left us feeling drained. And this on top of the traumatic months that had preceded it when we were facing and working out what to do about Daniel's initial regression into autism. As the hours of therapy reduced and Daniel spent more time in the nearby nursery, we should have been feeling as if we had more time and more energy to use. But what actually happened was that we collapsed into the space that these demands vacated, and felt unable to get up again. There were a few things that kept us going.

First and foremost, we had both been practising Heartfulness meditation[9] by that time for more than 10 years. It is actually Sahaj Marg that we practice, which is the full system from which Heartfulness comes. One valuable thing, we feel, about this particular meditation is

---

[9] http://en.heartfulness.org/

an aspect of it called transmission. What that is and how it works would be a theoretical discussion that I would not be able to do justice to, but the important thing is that this transmission can be felt within, often very tangibly, and often from the very start. Over time, the effect of it accumulates and has led to a permanent deep nourishing presence within us, which can be called upon at any time to provide a sense of well-being, even amidst the turbulences of life. In difficult moments, while not removing the difficulties, we have found that it very much helps us retain a greater perspective and balance than would otherwise be possible, In my own case, what I now recognise as significant traits of autism in myself in my youth, which made my teens and most of my 20s traumatic in many ways - only started to dissipate once I started this meditation, and I have now myself become a trainer in it. While our early experiences with Daniel's autism were extremely difficult for us and not at all easy to cope with, we recognise that the strain of them would have been very considerably greater without this meditation, and we are sobered when we see the shocking statistics about the numbers of families where autism occurs that eventually split.

Ours did not split, and there was never any question of it doing so, but it was put under a lot of strain even from the early months of Daniel's life, especially with the demands generated by his sleep and feeding issues. The programme at Mifne included couple's therapy as an integral part, and really seemed to bring us back together. But our return to England brought a gradual return to old habits, especially with the exhausting and intensive nature of the therapy. At the strong recommendation of Mifne, we continued with couples therapy (through Relate) here. It was helpful, but for some reason, in our case, didn't very quickly lead to fundamental change, and we needed to wait much longer for the re-emergence of peace and strong mutual trust and understanding.

On a more practical level, paying attention to things like diet and posture have been very helpful. It is tempting to eat junk when time is short and energy is low, but this compounds the problem. I have found that it is really worth reserving a little energy for healthy eating, as that energy will be more than repaid. With the disadvantage of many food sensitivities and long-standing stomach issues, this was important for me to focus on if I was to retain any ability to manage such a busy life. If I hadn't paid attention to what I was eating, these would have debilitated me, as they did at times. It was through being careful about what I ate, and monitoring what sorts of foods hurt me or helped me, that I have eventually arrived at a diet that has eliminated most of my stomach problems for the first time in over 20 years. In my case, this is a diet based largely on raw whole foods.

Posture is something that we were alerted to by our cranial osteopath. He recommended that we seek out videos of a woman called Esther Gokhale[10] (there are plenty on You Tube, including a useful practical talk she gave at TED). She has developed a surprisingly simple and easy set of techniques for, sitting, standing, lying, walking, bending, carrying things, etc. It is very easy to lose good posture when life is demanding and to slowly slip into a permanent slouch, which in turn drains energy and makes a positive attitude more elusive. Even as I type this book, I am sitting in one of the sitting postures she details in her book (*Eight Steps to a Pain Free Back*) and I can feel the difference it is making.

These have all been very helpful in coping with the intensity of our situation, and have reinforced the joy and hope that have come from the improved capabilities and emotional state we have seen in Daniel as a result of the therapy he has had.

---

[10] http://gokhalemethod.com/

Chapter 6 – Towards School

Daniel turned 4 in August 2013, and normally, he would have started in the Reception year at school the following month. This would have meant he would have been amongst the very youngest in his class, and we were quite nervous about this prospect, as he was still significantly behind in his social understanding. We weren't sure how he would fare cognitively either. We decided that we wanted to delay his entry to Reception by a year to give him extra time for development in order to maximise the chances of his feeling confident when he did start. He would still only just be the oldest in his class. Many people we spoke to about it told us how this was out of the norm and how they didn't encourage this sort of thing and how they couldn't be making exceptions all over the place and how it was a long and complicated application process that had to go through many stages of approval and was unlikely to be accepted in the end anyway. However, once we had chosen the school we wanted him to go to, it was actually very easy to arrange and they even did all the official bit for us.

So we did get that extra year to push forward with our own work with Daniel at home, and also with other therapies that we hoped would better prepare him for his entry to school.   Some of them were as follows.

We had already been taking him to hydrotherapy since shortly after we returned from Israel, and he had actually started it as part of his treatment over there.   As opposed to swimming lessons, hydrotherapy has more of an emphasis on helping him to be aware of his body in the water, and to gain the confidence to rely on his own judgements as regards his physical abilities and limitations. So it was not only about learning to support himself while swimming with bands or a float, but also about how to use the sides of the pool to guide him to the bottom of the steps, which in turn he had to feel for, lifting himself out of the pool; or about helping him to feel comfortable getting his face and hair wet, and so on.   It's not that he had any inherent physical disabilities, but he may have been limited in the understanding of how to use his own body and how to judge what is safe and what isn't.   Hydrotherapy has helped him a lot to develop this coordination, and once again we have been very lucky to have found an exceptional hydrotherapist who has built a strong relationship with Daniel.

CEASE is a detoxification approach based partly on homeopathy, which is designed to clear toxins out of the system.   While there were briefly clear positive and negative reactions on taking each course, we cannot be certain, with everything else that was going on, that this had any long term effect on him.   It is probably an example of some treatments having wildly different results for different people, and we were recommended CEASE by a family who felt that they had had phenomenal results with it.   For us, the results were not conclusive.

The same can be said of some of the bio-medical interventions that we have had.   With the very generous support of the Caudwell Children's Charity[11], which funds specific types of treatment for children with certain disabilities, we have tried several bio-medical approaches. Our first consultant was a name that was like gold-dust on the various parenting forums but who was extremely expensive, and we were very grateful to get the chance to go and visit him, as well as hopeful about what could come of it.   We filled in a very detailed questionnaire with details not only of Daniel's diet but also all aspects of his condition, and we were expecting a treatment that was based on all of this information and very specific to his individual needs.   We were disappointed to feel rushed, without much time to really discuss most of what we had written, and to be prescribed a standard generic food plan that seemed to be given out to everyone regardless of their

---

[11] http://www.caudwellchildren.com/

situation. It involved keeping to a very restricted diet, including the elimination of gluten and dairy. We were advised to do this for at least 6 months to see a difference. We did it for 8 months, but did not notice any change beyond the continuing improvements that we were already seeing from all the therapy. The reason we kept it up for so long is because I myself am not able to eat gluten, especially wheat, and was becoming increasingly intolerant of dairy (which I am now no longer able to take), and we do still try to limit his consumption of these things (and, especially, sugar), but cutting them out completely made life extremely difficult for Oksana, who was preparing most of his meals, so in view of the lack of perceived results, we re-introduced them. After that, we tried a different clinic, but sadly, the consultant there prescribed pretty much the exact same diet, and when we told her we had already done it for 8 months, she told us we should try it again anyway as it might have better results a second time. Judging from other parents' experiences, this seemed to be a very common diet that these bio-medical consultants prescribe, often irrespective of the issues of each individual patient. After this, we spoke with Caudwell and asked them if they could provide funding for a consultant who had more than one solution for their patients, and they gave us the complete list of clinics that they would be able to cover. We chose a naturopathic doctor in Central London at the Health and Wellness Centre[12]. On our first visit there, he very sensitively took a sample of blood from Daniel's thumb (Daniel was nervous, so we turned it into a game, with myself and Oksana each giving a drop of blood from our thumbs first, which made him willing to go through with it, albeit with a surprised and slightly offended "Aah" when the needle went in). He analysed it together with us, showing us the indications of various deficiencies in Daniel. From this, he understood what supplements Daniel needed, and used kinesiology (muscle testing) to understand what brands and quantities would be most suitable. We were not totally convinced about the kinesiology, but we were happy at least that the treatment this time was personalised and geared to our specific needs, rather than a general one-size-fits-all proposal. We have continued to visit this clinic, as Oksana, in particular, has felt that the supplements make a difference to Daniel (she is the one who usually administers them). She notices, for example, that his energy levels are lower on days when she forgets to give them to him. I have been doing some additional research on supplements lately, and have found out that the brands and forms of the vitamins that he sells to us when we go there are of a very high quality (which explains why they have a price to match), though I have also found that despite being labelled "Natural", the huge majority of

---

[12] http://www.nhwc.co.uk/

supplements on the market contain mostly synthetic ingredients, which can actually cause or worsen rather than prevent various health issues over years of long term use. Most Vitamin E on the market, for example, is derived from petroleum products. Even those labelled "Whole food-based" often begin with isolated or synthetic vitamins, which are then cultured with yeast, or simply placed in a tiny base of powdered food, whose ingredients are proudly listed in detail on the label. There are very few brands of supplements that use ingredients genuinely in their natural forms with the right co-factors in the correct proportions, and therefore able to be recognised by the body as nutrition, rather than alien chemical compounds. After more research, we are likely to re-assess which supplements we are giving to Daniel and switch to brands that are actually fully sourced from food, and therefore much more bio-available and risk-free.

Music Therapy was something we hadn't heard about, and we didn't have much of an idea of what it was when we eventually did hear people suggesting it. But we remembered that Daniel seemed to have something of an affinity to music in his early months, and felt that if nothing else, it would be nice for him to re-introduce that aspect into his life now. If the therapists could do something additional to help him more generally, that would be wonderful. Most of the music therapy sessions that we have had have been kindly funded, first by the charity,

Cerebra[13], and later by the Short Breaks programme from our local council. He now has Music Therapy sessions at school with a therapist visiting weekly from the Richmond Music Trust[14].

The first thing that struck us was that music therapy wasn't just about having fun with music. Each of the therapists he has had – there have been 4 so far – has had an impressive understanding of some of the more subtle social and other needs of an autistic child, and a great intuitive ability to establish a relationship with him and bring out some of his hidden potential. The emphasis has been on the therapist engaging in joint interactive music creation with Daniel. He is not, of course, required to understand music theory or know how to play any instrument; rather he is encouraged to make sounds with the instruments that will in some way accompany the sounds that the therapist makes with her instruments as she follows him with her music and invites him to "respond" to her musically. The idea is that through music and creativity, he may become able to reveal and develop confidence in his interest in and capacity for joint endeavours that it is not easy for him to exhibit in other situations. And that really does seem to be what has happened. Initially, he was only interested in

---

[13] http://w3.cerebra.org.uk/

[14] http://www.richmondmusictrust.org.uk/

experimenting with the various instruments alone and without much awareness of the therapist. Then he started to use the instruments to make elaborate and detailed stories that he insisted on telling at length without any opportunity for anyone to intervene . But as time has gone on, he has become more collaborative with the therapists and responsive in terms of participating musically in what they are doing. Rather than banging the drum as hard as he could, he started to be able to choose to use the instruments at different volumes and speeds, often in natural response to the lead from a therapist.

When he had developed familiarity and comfort with this, he was placed in a series of small groups with one or more other children. This has had mixed results due to the compatibility of the children in any group, which could not be guaranteed beforehand (though the combinations of children were carefully put together) and also because of the stage they were at in their development. For example, Daniel was going through a particular stage of social experimentation at one point, and was put in a group with a boy who was very sensitive to loud sounds. Unfortunately, Daniel began to enjoy banging the instruments especially hard, seeming to enjoy the boy's putting his hands over his ears when he did so - not being able to make the connection between this "funny" reaction and the discomfort that it was communicating - so that partnership was ended quickly. But there have been other groups where much positivity was displayed, where social skills were successfully encouraged and developed, such as taking it in turns to play something and being actively aware of what the other children are doing during their turns. Sometimes, a child might take longer to understand what they were to do and to get through it, and they learnt to be attentive and patient, and to show an appreciative reaction at the end. Daniel has even proactively suggested turn-taking games at times. We have been continually impressed with the quality and sensitivity of the therapists, who have all seemed to us to have a deep and intuitive ability to reach their children through music and bring out the best in them. This work continues in his school now, when he is in a group with one other pupil, and we are very happy with it. It is not the sort of therapy where you expect to see sudden breakthroughs in his daily life after a particular session – it is much more gradual and subtle than that - but the awakening of important skills is evident, at least in his progress during the sessions, and that in itself is a positive and hopeful indicator. We feel confident that music therapy is of great benefit to him.

The Davis Method[15] is only the second complete approach to autism we have come across that has really chimed with us and resonated with our own understanding of autism and how it relates to our son. The first was the

---

[15] http://www.davisautism.com/

Mifne method, which truly enabled Daniel to make the firm choice at a very early age that his life would be one of active engagement and participation in this world rather than one of retreat and separation from it; and it gave us the tools to support him as much as we could with the difficulties that come with that brave quest. We still use these tools on a daily basis, and whenever we are with him. We have, to the extent that we have been able, integrated them into ourselves and they are now a part of all our interactions with him. The Davis Method works with autistic children and adults of all varieties, but in our case, we are using it to fill in the gaps that remain in Daniel's social integration, primarily around his awareness of the distinctness of other individuals. Our relationship with it has been atypical and experimental in several ways, which I shall explain.

We first came across it via a recommendation from someone I met in Denmark through the meditation that we do, who has used it very effectively on her own autistic son, and who is now herself a facilitator and trainer of the method. She enthused about how it had helped her family, and recommended that we read an introductory book on it, *Autism and the Seeds of Change*, by the founder of the method Ron Davis. He had been severely autistic himself as a child and young man, unable even to speak in sentences until the age of 17, but has been one of the very few who recover by themselves with no apparent cause of the recovery. In his case, this development came from new understanding that he acquired through making clay model representations of his father and brother, who had used to beat and badly mistreat him. It seems that he had unconsciously been using the activity of making the models to process and understand what had gone on in the situations in which he was abused. Through doing this, he gradually understood the sequence of events that led to the beatings and what the warning signs were. Until then, this had not been obvious to him, as he had only been conscious of the immediacy of what was happening at any one moment, without any ability to conceptualise how events fitted together. He was then able to deduce his own part in this sequence (which he had previously not perceived), working out that he had had options, such as removing himself from the scene when warning signs began to occur. Having become awakened to this new understanding of how his world worked, he went on building on it, leading to an ability to not only become an active part of the world, but in his case, devising an entire programme to help other autistic people based on his own experience of autism.

What we really liked about it was that it is very simple and at the same time a very profound and respectful approach to the autistic person. It is not aimed at any sort of reconditioning or specific behavioural change. On the contrary, it is aimed at preserving the unique qualities of each person while allowing them to expand into areas of social understanding that have so far proven inaccessible. This enables them to relate more naturally and comfortably with the world around them. It was not, like so many other methods we have come across, about training the autistic person like a circus animal, offering praise or flimsy "rewards" to encourage desired behaviour but leaving the person with no real inner-understanding of *why* that behaviour is desired, which would be a much more satisfying and fulfilling motivation than a biscuit or a pat on the head. It was simply about gently and patiently introducing a series of simple concepts to the autistic person designed to awaken them to areas related to social perception that autistic people have often closed off. These were based on the experience that Ron Davis had as an autistic boy and the process he went through to awaken himself from the confusion and consequent impotence in which he existed. It begins with concepts that are so self-evident for non-autistic people that we take them for granted without even being consciously aware of them, unable to imagine that they could be missing in another person; but which autistic people generally lack. The first are what are classed as the 3 components of each person - mind, body and "lifeforce" (the latter representing our wants, needs and urges, and the motivation to act on them). It might seem difficult to believe that even an autistic person, especially one classed as "high functioning", could operate to any degree in this world without an inherent understanding of what a mind or a body are, or more importantly, how they go towards constituting a person, but Davis's experience (and many others') showed that there is actually no clear dividing line in an autistic person's mind between themselves and others. It is as if we are somehow all one indistinct entity without independent thoughts or wishes. Whether this is a failure to advance beyond the social consciousness of a baby or an indication of a very elevated spiritual condition (or both), it holds the autistic person back from living a balanced life here. In the Davis Method, these concepts are introduced in a fun way and then modelled in clay. Then, the therapist and the parents in the course of everyday life, use normal situations to reinforce these concepts naturally and lightly. It is very subtle, but works on the level of an inner-awakening of the autistic person, and can lead over time to significant changes and increased balance and orientation. These basic concepts are followed by others, also based on Davis's evolution from autism. They include Change, Time, Sequence, Cause and Effect, Consequence, and so on, all exemplified in the way he grew to understand his early life situation and his place in it. An example is his realisation that there were warning signs before unwanted things happened, and actions that he could have taken to change how the situations developed. The concepts also include Order and Disorder. Davis has explained how the transition from immersion in his internal autistic world to his emergence to engage with the outer world was characterised by a terrifying general experience of utter chaos all around him , which compounded the deep pain implicit in choosing to continually face the utter harshness of what is considered normal human interaction in the world, rather than remaining in retreat from it. The Davis Method is intended to provide understanding and support to the autistic person as they make this move towards integration in the world, while facilitating the conceptual awakenings that can allow them to grow. The concepts lay a foundation for and culminate in the final concept of Social Integration.

We came across the method in early 2014. Daniel was 4 and, we discovered, too small to work with the concepts beyond a light introduction the most basic ones. It is unusual to start them with a child younger than 6 or 7, and now that he is six and a half, we are looking to start a more in-depth phase of this work.

There are not many practitioners of this method in the UK, and most of them are not within reasonable travelling distance of us. After we had read the book and decided that we both felt that this was worth perusing, we did travel to meet a couple of practitioners, but we didn't feel we made a strong enough connection with them to have facilitated a good working relationship, so we decided not to take it forward at that time. But we were later put in touch, by the person who had originally suggested the method to me, with a very experienced facilitator in

Germany, who we instantly felt comfortable with and confident in. She has been a great support to us and has helped us significantly with many issues and general questions we have had about Daniel over the past couple of years. We have greatly valued her consistently compassionate and incisive input. She has supported us by Skype to be able to introduce the initial concepts to him ourselves, using clay. This is the first way in which our experience of this method has been experimental; it is usually done through face to face sessions between the practitioner and the autistic person. I would have to say that the element of using Skype to impart to us an understanding of how to facilitate the method to Daniel has not been completely successful. While we understand the basics of the Method, we do not feel confident in the intricacies of how most effectively to deliver it and to build on it after the sessions. Daniel has clearly absorbed some of the content and we do successfully use some parts of this to help him in daily life - for example, in appreciating that other people may like or want different things to what he likes or wants. But now that he is well into his 7th year, we decided together with the therapist that in order to fully benefit from the Method, he needed to have some face-to-face time with the her, and we flew her over from Germany to spend 3 days with us. It was an important decision and enabled us to better understand where Daniel was at this time, and what the next steps should be to be able to support him further.

She felt that he already had a grasp of most of the concepts we had introduced, and was too young to start on the more advanced ones (which he may never need to do, as he may well grasp them naturally when age appropriate), so we spent the time instead planning how we could best support him moving forwards. Cognitively, he is well in advance of his age, and she also noticed his deep caring and benevolent nature, but emotionally - in terms of his social awareness and confidence - he was functioning more at the level of a shy 2 year old than a 6 year old. A lot of this gap was to do with his not yet having developed the ability to feel his wants and needs and to express them with confidence Through all the work that has been done with him, he was showing promising signs of being ready to move forward quickly with this, and she felt that within a year or two, there was a very good chance that he will have closed the gap. The building blocks for his progress in this area - including his desire for it - were established now. But his confidence was low, due to his lack of experience. Even if there were no longer any intrinsic limitations to what was possible for him, the huge gulf between what his peers have been through and experimented with around this over the past 4-5 years and his own experience was a significant barrier. This is why he was still filling the space around him with words and long explanations about stories he was inventing. These are great strengths of his - his intelligence and creativity - and it was much easier for him to retreat into them without leaving any space for anything else than to step out into a new and untried area where there was much vulnerability. She suggested 3 subtle but powerful ways that we could support him in moving ahead.

The first relates back to the early "lifeforce" concept of the Davis Method, and the fact that Daniel has not yet succeeded in fully individuating himself from the rest of the world - identifying his own likes, wants and preferences in contrast to those of others, which he often absorbed as his. The chatter about his stories was also a way of avoiding an emotional way of relating (he did not always avoid this, especially in safe situations with us, but often) by relying on his cognitive strengths, and it invited us to respond to him on a cognitive level that he felt comfortable with. She told us to respond on a "lifeforce" level wherever possible, which essentially means responding to the energy he was bringing to the interaction rather than to the words or ideas he was saying. For example, we needed to pay more attention to how he was feeling, and if he was getting excited about part of a story he was enjoying, we would reflect that excitement both by briefly joining him in it and also by reflecting back to him that we had observed it, "I can see you're really enjoying this." We needed to start using language that focussed on his feelings, wants, and likes/dislikes, rather than on the content of what he said, so that he would slowly become more comfortable and experienced in these areas and not feel so overwhelmed by them that he needed to retreat into his (impressive) mind. This was a big change and required a new awareness of what was underlying his words. It also required the sensitivity to bring this shift in subtly, and not with any insistence or intensity that would cause him to recoil further from his feelings.

The second way was an even bigger change. It was to temporarily (for at least a few months) give him less imaginative ideas or suggestions in his play and in daily life. The therapist's observation was that when we proposed such ideas, Daniel let go of any wants that were emerging in himself. By holding off, we would be giving him the space to first experience, then express through words of behaviour, what he wanted to do next - for example, where he wanted his game to go, and thus to strengthen his confidence in expressing and standing up for his wants and ideas. Instead we were to join him with our full attention wherever he was with his play, and offer occasional commentary on what was happening and what Daniel was wanting and feeling. The rationale behind this is that autistic people are generally very susceptible to influences that come to them from outside, which they are almost unable to prevent absorbing or conforming to. We understood the logic, but this part is very hard. We have always used imaginative ideas as a very effective way of reaching him and connecting with him, and he has been very responsive to it. When he was very young and just emerging from the depths of his coping strategies, offering this sort of input was a vital part of inviting him to join us in the social world. But now, at this stage of his development, he needs the space, for a short time, to be able to assert his own wants and needs, and it is a constant challenge to fulfil this.

Finally, when we are in a playground or other social setting where there are other children, we should facilitate his interaction with them, but in a discreet way - not making too big a thing of it. For example, when the therapist was visiting, she simply mentioned to him that there was a girl in the playground that had looked at him and lightly suggested that she might want to play. She didn't put any pressure on him by expecting or suggesting that he do anything with that information; she simply mentioned it. And Daniel, demonstrating his current readiness and wish to connect with others, took the observation enthusiastically. He was delighted and went over to her and followed her around, trying to join in what she was doing. She was happy with this, though not particularly communicative. It was necessarily a little awkward, given his lack of experience, but the important thing was that he had a positive experience of social interaction with a peer and that it was his own experience. We did not intervene at all, and would only have done so, delicately, if there had been any sign of a significant problem. Even if his own experience had been a more difficult one, we could still have supported him and later (lightly) helped him to understand what had happened and what there was to learn from it. As it was, he was jubilant, coming over to us at one point and announcing, "this is a girl and she likes to play with me!"

We are currently implementing these strategies with support and feedback from the Davis Method therapist, and look forward to seeing the results of them.

The other way in which we have been experimental in our involvement in the Davis Method is that we have been part of some initial research into a new device called a NOIT[16], which has been developed by Ron Davis as an aid for autistic people who are transitioning to a new relationship with the world in which they are living. We are part of the trials of this device, which is to be worn on the upper back through the day, and is designed to give a sense of orientation and reduce the chaos that they experience around them. It brings them back from any urge they might have to retreat inwards, by emitting a particular ting sound to each of their ears simultaneously every few seconds. The idea is that it will support them during their treatment with the Davis Method, at the end of which they will be able to orient themselves naturally and will have no further need for the NOIT, and can be weaned off it. It can then be kept on hand for later use during

---

[16] http://www.noitresearch.org/

particularly stressful periods. The mechanics of how exactly that particular ting sound can be so effective escapes us, but it has seemed to work for us. After Daniel had been wearing it for about a year, we questioned whether it was making any difference and so removed it for some time. Within a few days, his behaviour became much more unfocussed and apparently disoriented, so we put it back and have been using it ever since. Being part of the trial, there have been some problems with the reliability of the device (which, especially at first, seemed to cut out intermittently) and with the effectiveness of the sticky pads that are used to attach it (which lasted often less than a day as opposed to the intended 7-10 days, though this may have been in part due to Daniel's small size and smaller back area compared with the mainly older children and adults who were trialling the NOIT), but they have been taking our feedback along with that of the other participants and working to improve on these issues.

The Davis Method is currently the primary tool that we are actively using to help Daniel.

We approached our search for a primary school for Daniel with heavy hearts. We had been keeping an eye out in the local area for good schools, but hadn't felt inspired with what we had seen. We resorted to looking at the Ofsted school rankings, and although there are far fewer primary schools than nurseries with the highest rating, which made a targeted search easier, we knew that this wasn't necessarily the best way to narrow down our search. Some schools which had earnt an "Outstanding" rating may not be anything special, but could be very tuned in to how to get through an Ofsted inspection successfully, while others with the next ranking down may be truly excellent schools that just didn't have the interest or understanding to know how most effectively to jump through the inspectors' hoops. But we used it as a guide. We expected that we would need to travel to enable Daniel to go to a suitable school, but we didn't know how far, and at that time, we simply didn't have the energy to pro-actively comb the whole area within a large radius to find something that may or may not be appropriate. We made a start at trying all the same. The first couple of schools we went to had specific provision for autism. One of them, which was actually not too far from us, had professionals there who could identify when a child with autism was struggling and work with them in an Autism Unit when required or on a regular basis to support them in their integration into school life. The other, a little farther away, had a wing which was devoted to autistic children, and where they were taught in much smaller groups by teachers who clearly cared a lot for them. We did seriously consider these schools for a while as it did seem that he would have good support there, but after a lot of consideration and advice, we decided against them for 2 reasons. The first was that Daniel was doing so well and showing so much potential to continue to do so that putting him in a special environment, however well designed and cared for, would have felt as if we were robbing him of the opportunity to rise to his full potential to integrate.   There was little mobility between the autistic wing and the rest of the school, and if he started school in the autistic wing, that's where he would finish.   Even if he became capable of moving to the mainstream part of the school, this wasn't generally done, so there wasn't the support structure to ensure the success of such a transition; and the later it occurred the more stark it would be   The second reason was that we didn't want him to feel defined by his autism. At 6 and a half, we very lightly introduced him to the word. He is approaching the age where he will begin to understand that there is something different about him (other children already sense that there is), at least in terms of his getting more individual care at school than other children, and this prompted us to lay the foundation for an eventual discussion about it, without making it a serious or big thing or presenting it as an important part of his composition.   We wanted to pre-empt any confusion he might develop about it in case it was brought to his attention in a less favourable way.   But for him to be taught in a special section of a school that is specifically for autistic children would invite him to define himself as autistic in a much more profound way, as would being regularly removed from class and taken to a unit called the Autism Unit.   He has autism, but the richness within him extends well beyond that label. We do not consider his autism to be the defining part of who he is, and we have always tried to avoid letting him feel limited by such a label.

So we went back to the drawing board, but fortunately, before we had got very far, a friend of ours told us that he was sending his son to a school we hadn't come across, which was within walking distance of where we lived, and which they were very happy with. So we went to visit it, along with Yael, and as soon as we walked through the door, we were all fairly certain that this would be the school we would choose for Daniel. Despite the less than ideal building that they were then occupying, they had clearly made impressive use of the space available and had created a free and spacious environment for their Reception children, yet one that had an inherent calmness and sense of order. The children were both extremely disciplined and evidently very contented to be there, and they were all actively engaged in the lessons throughout. The activities were educational, while also being fun, and the children naturally and effortlessly navigated their way through them, having been well prepared for each one. There was none of the sense of being in an "institution" that we had felt in some of the other schools we had visited; there was a freshness, optimism and enthusiasm, and it was easy to see that the staff were continually striving for better ways to serve the children. We hadn't expected to find anything like this so close to our home, and were not only delighted with the school we had found, but relieved that we would be able to avoid long and difficult daily commutes without compromising on the quality of the school.

Apart from the terrible but isolated incident recounted in the last chapter about one of Daniel's early visits to the school, our relationship with them in preparing him for life there was very positive. We met with the headmaster several times, who assured us that a suitable teaching assistant would be found to give dedicated support to Daniel, even though the funding from his Statement would not necessarily cover it in full. I was asked at one point whether we would prefer an assistant with expertise in autism but who may not be the best match for Daniel, or someone who wasn't an expert but who was warm, open, ready to build a nurturing relationship with him and willing to learn about the particular challenges that his autism presented for him. It was a loaded question, but fortunately, our thinking was exactly along these lines, and they did assign someone to Daniel for his Reception year who supported him wonderfully and who he warmed to very much. He actually still talks about her half way through Year 1. They hadn't been sure until the summer that it would be her, so they sent his teacher and a few potential assistants to come and visit him at home to start to play with him and make a relationship with him in the months before he started, and we are sure that having that familiarity with a good portion of the staff who would be around him made his transition to school much easier. In the event, he coped with it much better than many children without any special needs.

This preparation also helped him to rebuild a positive attitude towards school, and he decided well in advance of starting there in September 2014 that he would throw himself enthusiastically into it, which he did. We had been worried that academically he might be far behind the other children, which might shatter his confidence. He was, but the support that the school builds in to its methods ensured that it wasn't something that shook or disadvantaged him. He was continually encouraged and believed in, and the great effort that he determinedly put in to be able to stay with and participate in daily activities at school meant that the gap between him and the others was not as big as it could have been. We do not believe that the gap arose from any issue with his cognitive abilities, which we now appreciate are strong, but resulted from a degree of being overwhelmed by the relatively busy and public nature of the setting. As he began to adjust to this, his academic performance rose to close to the norm, then to the lower end of the norm, and is now at or in some areas above the norm, and still improving. He loved both his teacher and especially his dedicated assistant in his Reception year, and they repeatedly reported improved confidence at school. He even started volunteering to stand up and answer questions, and displaying appropriate and spontaneously playful behaviour.

However much he loved his school though, there was a change in him after he started. While being totally focussed and expending every effort to make the most of his school life, he began to display more disoriented, volatile and repetitive behaviours again at home. It was as if he had given all he had at school, and had no energy left with which to focus for the rest of the day. Occasionally, he even started wetting himself again, and always at school, which indicated something was wrong, but without any other indication, it was not always evident to staff that he was in a state of distress if he didn't choose to volunteer this. Worse, while maintaining his positive attitude to all aspects of school life, including all of his classmates, there were clearly some aspects of the social life of the school that were difficult and unsettling for him. He became very disturbed by little things that happened that he imagined to be bullying. Often these were just friends joking around with him, but in a way that was not understandable to him as such, and that he experienced as threatening. Other times, there was some aggressive intent: one evening he came back from school and was fighting everything that we said or did. I asked him whether anything had happened at school, and he told me, with tears welling up, that one of his friends had said that he would smash up his scooter so that he wouldn't be able to go to school any more, adding in distress, "and that would be very sad." Another time, that same child had told him that he would eat Daniel's mummy and daddy leaving him all alone with no-one to look after him, which, of course, was much more disturbing for him. These may be the sorts of thing that children routinely throw backwards and forwards to each other in fun in the course of school life, but for an autistic child of inherent goodwill, exposure to such willful malice, however mild, is bewildering, painful and completely destabilising even when observed between others; all the more so when they are the subject of it. The last thing they could bring themselves to do would be to participate in it and throw similar rocks back. Becoming a perpetrator themselves would go against the grain even more, and would make even less sense to them. Sadly, their inability to do so, and their profound shock in such situations, makes them susceptible to being subject to further instances, and eventually to real bullying. It is a bind that affects many autistic children, and it is one that there doesn't seem to be any easy answer to. We tried to be especially understanding and containing to him during these periods, and even briefly re-introduced some sessions in the room to help him to process it. It remains an area where he has much uncertainty, though he is perhaps making some strides. He has been much more settled in his second year of school (Year 1). He still talks about what happens regarding social relationships at school with some difficulty, though the stories now are not so much about things that others have done to him, and are much more symbolic. There is a particular boy who he says is so violent that the teachers are all frightened of him: he throws rocks and knives at them all and is continually sent to the Headmaster's office, but the Head is terrified of him and runs away to hide before he gets there. We are not sure what exactly he is processing with such tales (which are, obviously, not true and have been the source of some amusement when we have discussed them with staff), but at least he is not a victim in them, even when we ask him specifically about this.

The school has provided excellent support to him. They seem to have an infrastructure that facilitates the keen and continual observation of the needs of all children, and they run many interventions, that are open to all children, in several of which Daniel has partaken. The latest has been an initiative called Talk-Boost. A small group of children spends half an hour together during the lunch-break 3 times a week and they play games and activities designed to encourage their social awareness and appreciation of others. They take turns, play games in which they rely on each other, and enjoy activities such as one of them being sent out of the room while the other 3 make a list of things they like about that child, which they can share with her when she returns. It gives them practice and experience of giving and receiving affirmation from peers. It sounds like a very valuable group. Other interventions might be much shorter and more focussed on a particular academic need in class.

So, once again, good fortune has rescued us from the difficulties that many families with autistic children have, this time around school. In fact, the only issues we have ever had with the school have been around communication, and this has been in both directions. As with the nursery, we may have jumped in too keenly with questions about what was happening in the early months when Daniel's behaviour at home was seeming to indicate distress. Our intention was never anything other than constructive collaboration, but our worry may have prevented us from balancing our questions with the necessary acknowledgement and appreciation of what they were doing for him. It was once fed back to us that we could sometimes come across as overly direct or overbearing (especially by email), which shocked us, as this had never been our intention or attitude, but there was obviously a reason why we were perceived as such. We accepted this feedback and began to be more careful to ensure that our communication represented more accurately the fullness of what we wanted to express. In turn, we fed back that we needed more visibility and feedback about what was happening with Daniel at school so that we could effectively work together with the staff to help him, and to input into any observations they made or strategies they used. We wanted a collaborative partnership with them, but felt that we were being told only the positive and that any issues or uncertainties that the staff had (and we would have expected there to be some uncertainties arising from learning to manage his condition) were not shared with us. We felt less informed than we would have liked to be about his needs and achievements at school, and how they were being addressed, and in the dark about what level of support he was actually receiving - it was clearly less than the dedicated one-to-one support that we had been promised, but we were only discovering this by putting together the pieces from what we picked up here and there. It may have been changed for good reason, but we wanted to be informed about this, and ideally involved in the decision. We also feared that our requests for information about the nature and level of the support he was getting were either considered intrusive or demanding, or taken as complaints, when in fact neither is the case. This was all accepted by them, and we were promised a real "thought-partnership" which worked for the rest of the year, but has needed to be re-established after the annual changeover of staff that takes place at the start of each academic year. I'm sure we will get to a more permanent communication solution with the school, and it is improving. There is a much greater mutual openness now and happiness to discuss such things collaboratively and even to understand what Daniel's development process is at home and how this might be supported in school. And most importantly, we trust that any changes that have taken place are appropriate, whether or not we are consulted or kept informed of them, as we see the consistent enthusiastic commitment of the school to Daniel's individual needs, as to those of all the children, though of course we would much prefer to be pro-actively kept in the loop and involved in the decisions, as we do have a valuable perspective to bring. They are constantly monitoring him, helping him where needed, and keeping abreast of what he needs next, doing what they can to provide it. There is an excellent assistant who understands him very well and spends several slots a week with him in class (and who he loves). And they are constantly seeking ways to challenge him and move him forward. Very recently, he was invited to give a talk about space and the solar system to his class, which he prepared thoroughly. He was able to deliver it clearly and answer decisively questions that the other children had. It was wonderful for his confidence, and as an experience of appreciation by his peers. In all of this, we have been luckier than many parents of children with special needs, who have less visibility of what goes on at their child's school, less willingness from the school to collaborate, and far fewer reasons to be able to trust their school to do the best for their children. Indeed, our Davis Method therapist has said that in all her experience of working with autistic children, the child never gets everything they need from school to best support their development. So in this respect, we are very grateful for the extent to which this school looks after our son.

Chapter 7 – Where We Are Now

Our odyssey through Daniel's autism to date has been an unconventional one, even by the standards of those who have a tendency to seek alternatives. I cannot explain why everything seems to have fallen into place for us so fortuitously and how we have come across in particular two obscure treatments that have offered so much hope and been so much in line with our own underlying approach to Daniel's condition. What the Mifne and Davis methods have in common, and that is so rare to find, is the readiness - the insistence, even - to meet the autistic child where they are, to fully accept and value them as they are; to nurture their inner potential so that they can learn to navigate their environment and grow into fulfilled beings. They both have a firm and unwavering belief, based on repeated experience, that the child within is much richer than what we can see from the outside, and actually much more so than we could imagine. They both work at the child's level - bringing out in them what they find inside, with an emphasis on giving them a feeling of genuine well-being that will encourage them to open up - rather than imposing on them a targeted set of behaviours that would most likely be meaningless to them and do nothing to alleviate the suffering that they are undergoing. And they both have a confidence, based on consistent results, that they can profoundly help each child, and a clear knowledge of how to do it. We have not found any other treatments that have these characteristics. There may possibly be more out there, but they are not easily found, and to have come across 2 of them in this short period is incredible.

We still have a job to do to build on what we have learnt, and to keep ourselves fresh and active in the evolving process. New challenges arise at each stage of Daniel's growth and continue to surprise us, and we need to stay tuned in to him to understand where he is really coming from. It is so easy to mistake his motivation at times and deal with things in the wrong way. Recently, he went through a phase of making silly noises all the time, which he had learnt from classmates at school. When we asked him to stop, he would laugh at us and continue with the noises as if in defiance. We thought this was a disciplinary issue, which we have never really had to worry about before, and on the advice of many, we introduced a "thinking chair" that he had to go and sit on for a fixed time to think about his behaviour. At the end of that time, he said, "I have thought about my behaviour, and I think it was nice." Fortunately, this woke us up to the fact that this wasn't a disciplinary issue at all. He was not challenging us by not giving us the answer we were expecting. In fact, he never has. He was just being transparently honest. For him, it *was* nice to make those sounds, and putting him on a chair to think about it must have been a surreal development for him. He couldn't have known that we had a particular perspective in mind that we wanted to impose on him, and even if he had, he wouldn't have had any idea how he could get there (though I'm sure he would have tried). So we had to revert to the ways we had always chosen to use.

It was a vital lesson for us. Treating something as a matter of discipline when it is not could be devastating for our relationship with our child. It unnecessarily puts us on opposing sides, when enmity is so crushingly painful for him, and it leaves him feeling (correctly) that he hasn't been understood. It would be so easy for a situation like that to escalate and for the mutual opposition to intensify and solidify. Even when peace was later made, a sadness and sense of alienation would remain, which, if repeated, could poison our whole relationship and undermine all the work we have been doing.

That is not to say that there is no place for laying

down rules.   We have used the chair very occasionally for pre-defined situations, and there does need to be the understanding that if Mummy or Daddy tells him to do something, then he has to listen and do it.   But we do not have (and do not want) the "luxury" of freely expressing ourselves with unfiltered annoyance.   This would undermine rather than enhance any discipline, as the harshness of our behaviour would become central and dominant in his experience of the situation and he would necessarily lose sight of what the issue was originally about. Instead, we make it very clear, in a non-oppositional way, what circumstances will result in having to sit in the chair and for how long (usually they relate to a particular behaviour that he is already working to change, or to ignoring what we say), and if those situations arise, we first remind him of what he is doing.   This is not to "give him another chance", but to make him conscious of something he is not currently conscious of.   When he becomes conscious of it again, he very often acts on this consciousness, as he is always well motivated to do the right thing.   On the rare occasions when he persists, we remain supportive to him, and in that supportive vein, we direct him to the chair.   We do not make him feel shame or guilt, and we never criticise him.   Those things would be devastatingly counter-productive.   Instilling an idea in him that there is something wrong with him or that he is inherently incapable of doing what we want would not only shatter his evolving self-confidence, but would also guarantee repetition of the undesired behaviour: if he absorbed from us the belief that he was just not able to do what we wanted, what would happen to his incentive to try? He would give in to the inevitability of repeating the behaviour because we have given him the message that he won't be able to stop it even if he does try. It could so easily lead to a destructive cycle of conflict and further loss of mutual understanding. As parents, it is such an easy trap to fall into, but one that it is imperative to avoid, especially with autistic children, who are much more profoundly hurt by any hint of a conflict, and are devastated to find themselves involved in one through no intention of their own.

Actually, Daniel's belief that his behaviour was nice after thinking about it arises from his ongoing difficulty in perceiving himself as separate from other people and with distinct wishes. If he is behaving in a loud way when we are not well, for example, and we ask him, "I have a headache - do you think I am happy to hear those loud noises?" He might answer, with complete honesty, "Yes, I think you are happy to hear them." His own positive experience of them is the only one he can conceptualise. We are working with him at the moment using the Davis Method on the understanding that other people have distinct thoughts and different preferences, and he is getting to the stage where he can easily be led to this understanding in many circumstances, but often, it still does not come spontaneously. Similarly, unless someone's facial expressions are unusually clear, he is still unable to read the subtleties of their reactions to things. If we ask him whether a teacher liked something he did, he will say, "I don't know because she didn't tell me." We are learning together to get clues from people's faces, and he enjoys playing games where he has to say something silly and understand from our faces and body language what we feel about these ideas.

He is exceptionally trusting, believing everything we say - even if we tell him in play that we are going to eat him or throw him down the stairs. He will suddenly get upset, and if we then ask him, "Daniel, do you think I would really throw you down the stairs?", he will reply, "Yes, I think you will throw me down the stairs." It is as if the experience of the moment over-rides everything he knows about us. He has been very literal in his understanding of things, as well. Until recently, if we said something like, "your food is waiting", he would reply instantly that, "food is not alive. It can't wait." So we started playing a game called *Literally or Figuratively* (not 2 words that you would typically expect to use with a 6 year old) with 2 of his toy animals. One of them would say something like, "I'm so thirsty I could drink a big cup of water." and the other would say, "I'm so thirsty I could drink all the water in all the rivers in England.". Daniel would have to work out which was literal and which was figurative, usually finding the figurative one very funny. Then we would talk about why the figurative one was used at all and what it was attempting to convey. Finally, he would come up with his own examples for his animals and I would have to guess which was literal and which figurative. This game quickly led to an increased tolerance of figurative language.

Sometimes, though, it is as if he has a blurred understanding of the boundary between fantasy and reality. Currently, he is fascinated by space. He has an excellent understanding of the solar system and the history of the Earth, and easily absorbs difficult information and concepts from books and documentaries about it. Then he applies what he has learnt to imaginary ideas, drawing fascinating and impressive pictures of Mercury and Mars with geological activity happening at a rapid pace, creating an atmosphere and the beginnings of life. He says this is not just a story, it is true, and scientists have just not discovered it yet (it has happened since they last took pictures of those planets). Another picture he drew shows the whole solar system, with as yet undiscovered planets, and even a twin star, much bigger than the Sun, which we can't see as it is permanently obscured by the moon(!). Recently, he has compiled a picture book depicting in some detail the history of a planet where elephants reign, and which is in a different and much bigger Universe. He explains these a great length and in intricate detail, and doesn't like to be interrupted while doing so. Once imagined, as far as he is concerned, these are factual. Based on previous patterns, though, he is likely eventually to evolve the ability to discriminate between reality and imagination.

As with many, if not most, autistic children, Daniel's greatest remaining difficulty is with social understanding, and many of the issues already related in this chapter are a part of this. It is most notable, however, at school and with his friends, where there is still a big and very evident gap between his and others' conceptions of how to interact; and at gatherings like birthday parties, where Daniel has a lot of fun, but it is usually on his own and not conscious of, or at best not fully comprehending, the social existence of the other children. It is hard to know what to do to help him with this. We continue to use symbolic play to process concepts and events, and he continues to partake in interventions and activities at school designed to bring out his interest in others in a positive and experiential way. He is moving forward in this area, but not at a rate that is significantly reducing the gap between himself and other children. Social understanding cannot be forced, and if it is too relentlessly drummed into him, he will soon understand that something is wrong and will absorb some heaviness around it, making it more difficult to address in a natural and positive way. At present, we are doing what we can, as is his school, and beyond that, we are optimistic that the observations and suggested strategies of our Davis Method therapist will slowly fill in these gaps and empower him to approach social situations with more ease. It is interesting that when we have been in overwhelmingly positive environments where other children have behaved towards each other with only warmth, kindness and consideration (such as at the meditation centre we occasionally visit in India), he has responded by coming out of himself and behaving naturally and with ease. He thrives in such environments as they resonate with his ideals and his nature, and we strive to reproduce as many aspects of them as we can in daily life.

He has become more confident in expressing these ideals in the last year or so. At school some months ago, the children were given an exercise where they had to choose a super-power that they would love to have. He didn't seem interested in this, and rejected all of the suggestions that were put to him about being strong or fast or clever or able to see through walls and so on. As we were about to give up, he found one super-power that did attract him - the power to make other people happy. When we came up with that, he suddenly became interested in the exercise and in being "happy man". More recently, he decided that he didn't want to buy anything with the money he had collected to fill his money box, as he already had everything he needed. Instead, he wanted to give it all to charity. He asked us lots of questions about which charities help which groups so that he could make a decision about where his money would work best. Now that he has done a project on the rainforest at school, he is very concerned about the environment and interested in finding alternatives to burning fuels and reducing our material needs so that plants, animals and people do not need to go through the suffering that climate change is bringing about. He has not been subjected to any additional influence to push him in these directions; they have been entirely on his own initiative. And although we are both vegetarian, we have always been clear that he will be able to eat meat if he chooses to. However, he has always adamantly refused this idea, stating emphatically that "animals are our friends!" He has been genuinely saddened to learn that other people in our family do eat meat. His caring nature even extends to plants, which he can't bear to see hurt in any way.

And he puts this kindness into action in daily life, constantly looking for ways to support the people around him. Recently, during a very stressful and busy period, Oksana was anxious and tearful about how little time there was to do the things she needed to do that day. Picking up on this, Daniel calmly and pro-actively reassured her that everything was okay, repeatedly reaching out to her and trying to find ways to make her feel better, like offering the one remaining seat on the train to her rather than sitting in it himself. All of this is a reminder of his inner qualities, as discussed in chapter 4, which are now finding the space to start to emerge into the open.

We are very far from the end of the story - there is still a lot to do, especially in the areas of social interaction and of his incessant chatter about his favourite subjects, which we are now working on based on our Davis therapist's suggestions. But given where we started from, when it looked inevitable that Daniel would have a condition so serious he would need to be withdrawn from daily life and permanently subject to professional care, we are extremely grateful for where we are now, which would have been inconceivable when he turned 2. He is a consistently happy, trusting, and sincere boy, with a great personality, a brilliant and creative sense of humour, a fierce intelligence and is capable of showing and even asking for affection. Despite his age, he has impressive integrity and a set of values that most of us would aspire to but find unachievable. He is kind, firm and resolute in wanting the best for everybody, and is genuinely a joy to be with. And we are able to approach him with an infinitely better understanding of what life must feel like from his perspective, so we are better equipped to offer him meaningful support and less likely to deepen his anxiety with our clumsy reactions (though this may still happen at times).

I have tremendous respect and admiration for Daniel. Despite the difficulty of doing so, he has retained the innocent, loving and sensitive nature that he had as a baby, and which eventually led him to cut himself off from a world whose culture clashed painfully with it. After all of the support that we have been so improbably fortunate to receive, he has felt able to decide, however hard it is, to remain open and engaged with the world around him, while not compromising his inherent qualities; and he has enthusiastically thrown himself into it. It has been a courageous choice, and it leaves him exposed to much potential pain through his life. But with adequate self-esteem, confidence and positive coping strategies, with which we are striving to provide him, I believe he can not only become more resilient, but can prove to be even more of an asset to this planet than he already is. I look forward to standing with him on the next stage of his journey.

Afterword - 5 Principles

Daniel's transformation has been remarkable, and the soft loving nature that has slowly re-emerged in him since our visit to Israel in 2011 supports the proposal I put forward in chapter 4 that within each autistic child lies an angel. I would extend this to say that within every child, and even every adult, lies an angel, but the difference is that the autistic person, unlike the rest of us, cannot lose sight of their angelic ideals and engage in acts of cruelty or destruction to "stay afloat" in a competitive world. This is their stunning strength and - in the current environment - it is their great vulnerability. As a result of their integrity, they are judged, even by those closest to them, as in some way deficient and hopeless rather than understood for who they are. Even we, their carers, often assess them based on the expectations of the world rather than on their own criteria. Coupled with their extreme sensitivity to others' emotions and to sensory stimuli, they are faced with an intolerable situation that forces them to rely on coping strategies which might not otherwise be necessary. It is a self-fulfilling prophecy: we judge them to have weird anti-social behaviours and thereby create the conditions around them to reinforce their dependence on these behaviours.

Once we appreciate this and keep sight of the human being that we are dealing with - seeing their inner character rather than their exterior behaviour as their defining aspect - then we can help to empower them to bring about huge positive changes in themselves. If they lapse into coping mechanisms - like rocking or feeling dependent on fixtures in their surroundings or routine because the world is too much for them to manage on their own, we can learn to reassure them that they don't need to manage it on their own. We are there to support them, and they can trust us to consistently understand them and safeguard their interests. In our own experience, when this happens, they slowly they begin to depend more on us and less on their coping strategies. Even the sensory difficulties become much reduced and better managed, as does the anxiety in unfamiliar situations, as they no longer feel alone. They can trust someone else to understand and look out for them, and thereby gain the space to regroup themselves and build the strength to gradually become more independent. Could it really be so simple to revolutionise the quality of someone's life - just to offer them care, understanding and support? It seems to be that way, though putting this into practice effectively in the face of the prevailing expectations and judgements can be far from simple.

What we have learnt through the treatments we have found has truly revolutionised Daniel's life as well as our family's, but has required great commitment and vigilance to implement consistently during the course of daily life. As time has gone on, we have seen the results multiply, convincing us even further that this course is right and effective. But it is still very easy to deviate from it in difficult, busy or exhausting times.

It has helped us to bear in mind some of the core principles of what has been outlined in this book, to help us maintain our approach. Here are 5 of them:

Respect Who He is

This speaks for itself. It is simply about valuing our son regardless of what others expect from him or how they might judge him. Once we started looking for the positive within him, not only was there so much to see that we could easily have missed, but just through the process of valuing him, he was encouraged to be freer to express his true qualities. When we note behaviours that are more difficult to deal with, rather than trying to shut them down, we recognise them as coping mechanisms – crutches that it would be devastating to kick away - and we try to better work out what purpose they are serving. For example, if he is getting anxious at changes in routine (and thankfully, this has been much less of an issue for us than it could have been, as we were encouraged from the time he was 2 to give him as much experience of variation as possible), we will not demand that he absorb the situation and control his behaviour. We will try to recognise his distress as an indication that he is anxious about something changing. Then we will try to reassure him, verbally or by manifesting our own comfort with the change, and by giving him as much notice of upcoming changes as possible, presenting them as something to look forward to rather than something one needs to be braced for. That way, although changes still happen, he is partially protected from the uncertainty around them, and has less cause for anxiety. Or, if he seems to be getting over-excited and jumping around a lot after a friend has visited, we don't dismiss the excitement as "too much", demand that he behave in a more "appropriate" way and thereby not only force him to carry the unprocessed emotions about the visit, but also burden him with an experience of harshness that is profoundly painful for him and with the feeling of being responsible for causing us inconvenience, leaving him to conclude that his natural innocent behaviour is problematic. Instead, we try to understand this animation as a way of dealing with and expressing the happy but overwhelming emotions he is feeling about having been with his friend, and to react with a smile and some words that echo his emotional condition. If we do this, then not only do we get a happier son who feels more understood and connected, but there is a real chance that over time, his behaviour will become more "normalised" quite naturally. We have seen this happen in many areas. It is as if the sense of being fully and unconditionally accepted somehow soothes him on a deep level and gradually reduces his anxiety and sensitivities. But we do not react in this way simply because we want to bring about such changes - it is because we feel it is the right and respectful way to be with him. If these changes do happen, they will not be immediate - they will require a lot of patience, and there is no guarantee that they will happen at all. We still choose to try to respect our son because it is the only way that makes any sense to use now.

Have Patience

Things happen slowly. At times it may look as if nothing is changing, or even as if things are going backwards. When Daniel has been in phases of returning to repetitive behaviours, it may have felt ineffective even to increase the amount of therapy we were putting in. In retrospect, it might look as if the extra therapy was effective quite quickly, even after a matter of days. But during those days, when there was little evident response to our efforts, it was easy to lose heart.

Particularly at these times, but even in more positive times, it has been necessary for us to have patience not only with the process, but also with Daniel himself in those moments when he appears not to respond to it or to what we are saying to him. We also need to be able to give him time to respond to our questions, suggestions and invitations. As we learnt at Mifne, he often needs processing time to understand what is being proposed to him, to put it in the context of the situation and to work out his response to it. More generally as well, it is so helpful not to have expectations of him - simply to offer what we can and allow the process to take its course. If we have expectations, even when unexpressed, these will be unconsciously transmitted to him and he will pick up on them. When he does, he is much more likely to feel bad about not being able to meet them and to give up on trying, feeling it to be too big a mountain to climb to overcome what he will inevitably experience as our disapproval. We have needed at such times simply to give our best and let things take their course.

This doesn't mean that we shouldn't research other ways to get help for him or reach out to others who may have been through something similar. These, too, are crucial strategies, and we are always on the lookout for new ideas and approaches and insights. But if we can do this from an acceptance of where Daniel is now and of the process that it is necessary for him to go through in order to develop, it can be much more effective than a desperate quest based on panic and anxiety, which would negatively affect our daily interactions with him.

At the time of writing this, he is going through a prolonged phase of talking incessantly about stories that he is creating in his mind. Although he is directing his speech at us and interacting with us when we join him in discussing these subjects, the sheer amount of words he uses and his insistence on staying on the subject whatever is going on around him is often quite overwhelming for us, and we are not able to stay focussed on what he says. At these times, it is so easy to just switch off and stop listening, and let him just get on with it. Sometimes we do find ourselves doing that. But we are trying to increase the amount of quality time we spend with him, inviting him to other activities, and this does often have some effect. Above all, we are trying (and so far failing), to understand what the underlying issue is that he is worried about, so that we can work with him to help him overcome it. Sometimes the patience needs to be with ourselves and with the process as a whole – accepting that we don't always know what is going on and that we need help from people with a like-minded approach to identify what is happening and what we can do to support him.

So we are not seeing it as a crisis or something that

is likely to still be an issue in the months or years ahead, and we are not being hard on ourselves for not being able to address it by ourselves, but we do understand that we need to find some additional input to be able to help us with this. It is this issue as much as anything else that has prompted us to intensify our application of the Davis Method. While we have actions or possibilities available to us that are giving us hope, we have the luxury of being able to be more patient with this process. It is patience that allows us to conduct ourselves with Daniel in a way that inspires him to understand on a deep level that everything is going to be fine.

Trust

Trust is what makes such patience possible; trust that whatever happens is fine. Without an underlying understanding that Daniel's path will be what it has to be (after our best efforts), we will not be able to acquire that trust. Without it, it is easy to become despondent, to feel that things will never improve and that there is nothing we can do, and so to give up.

It is a delicate balancing act. On one hand, we need to accept the situation that we have and that our son has. There is no point in continually lamenting it and trying, in a desperate panic, to refute it or find a quick "solution" to it. This non-acceptance of the situation and our negative judgement of the nature of his existence that is implicit in it would only make him feel like more of a problem. It is only by accepting what cannot be changed and not trying to fight it that we can provide him with an appropriate environment for him to feel contained and supported.

But we don't yet know what can and what can't be changed, so on the other hand, we do need to be looking at everything we can do to help him, and finding other interventions that we feel can help. These are not mutually exclusive attitudes, and it is important to keep both. All it means is accepting what can't be changed and working hard on what can. What we are accepting is not that the current level of his difficulties will continue. What we are accepting is the situation - whatever will be - after we have done our best to help. We are accepting this in advance because it is this that cannot be changed, and not accepting it would be akin to not accepting him, which would be the worst and most destructive influence we could bring to our son.

If we can attain and keep this balanced attitude, it allows us to approach his difficulties without a counter-productive intensity or anxiety, and without complacency.   Anxiety on our part would undermine and pollute his self-image, while complacency would rob him of opportunities for improvement in his situation.   Instead, we can become able to accept him as he is, and at the same time offer him the best chances of an improvement in his quality of life.   This attitude in itself is something that can enrich his life and remove from it the common pitfalls of disappointment.

Contain

All of the above (and much of what is in this book) constitute containment.   I have written about it so extensively that it doesn't feel as if there's much more to say.   It is basically making him feel safe and secure in an environment which is, by its nature, threatening to him. We cannot do this by telling him things that we don't believe ourselves or presenting ourselves as happy or calm or accepting when that is not what we feel inside.   As a very sensitive and perceptive child, he will instantly feel that something is wrong.   He will not be able to formulate the concept that "Daddy's words and behaviour do not accurately reflect his current emotional state" but he will intuitively sense that he cannot trust what I am saying, even if he is not sure quite why, and will also experience me as someone whose words might not always be what they seem.

As well as being, from my current perspective, the most critical piece in aiding the transformation of an autistic child, containment also requires the most fundamental change on the part of the parent or carer. In order to make the child feel safe and secure, we need to feel safe and secure, both for ourselves and for them. If something has gone wrong and he cries and I feel so sad and helpless for him and hug him with my own tears of pain, that might make him feel loved, but not safe or secure. He will know that I feel helpless and will understand from it that there is nothing to be done - no hope - and that his environment is full of unexpected pitfalls that he has no idea how to navigate and that the people who care for him most and who he relies on cannot navigate either. This will fuel his distress and anxiety. If, by contrast, I hug him with compassion for his distress but without too much distress of my own, and instead with a conviction that he has the strength and resilience to overcome whatever has happened, that I can help him with it and that he might even learn to grow stronger through it; then he is bound to absorb at least some of that conviction.

Containment cannot be faked. It requires complete authenticity, because anything inauthentic will be effortlessly detected. And this is why it entails the greatest commitment from us. We cannot simply tell him or show him how we want him to feel. We need to make ourselves feel what we want him to feel. At first, this may seem to require the highest possible level of self-mastery, but with time, we have realised that this is actually how we really want to feel anyway. We are usually tempted to give in to worries and negative emotions, but we can't honestly say that that's where we want to be. Having an eye on containment gives us the opportunity to steer ourselves back to where we feel more comfortable.

In difficult moments, this can slip, though it is often in such moments that containment is more important. The Davis Method has a quick deep breathing process called "release" that is intended to bring us back to our centre so that we can take control of ourselves again in the midst of such situations. We combine this with the idea of "remembrance" from Heartfulness, that allows us to re-connect ourselves with the underlying presence that has evolved in the heart through years of meditation. They are powerful tools that make a huge difference when it is most needed.

Essentially, containing means managing ourselves to ensure that our own experience of the world is calm, positive and confident, as this is the only way to instill this much needed condition in our son.

Be Kind To Ourselves

Containment includes another way that we need to manage ourselves, and that is to go easy on ourselves, not expecting too much and not being hard on ourselves if things do not go to plan. Providing the best for a child, especially a very sensitive one, entails constant demands on our time, energy and even our thoughts and attitudes. There is not much space to just collapse and rest and look after ourselves. In all of this, we need to accept that we are human beings with human limitations, and simply cannot achieve best practice all of the time.

I have tried to make this book as useful as possible by discussing at length the strategies we have implemented to help our son. In doing so, I may have given the impression that we are exemplary parents with no failings or shortcomings. I haven't written at any length about the times when we have just not had the energy to keep it up, and have left him to play by himself or watch cartoons; or have half-heartedly gone along with whatever he was playing, unable to respond in more than a semi-conscious way to his wonderful enthusiasm; or have argued between ourselves and then just been flat and miserable for hours afterwards. It is inevitable that there will be such moments. Nobody would be able to maintain consistent excellence in such a task. It is vital to be able to understand when we are at our limit, and allow ourselves to take time out, without feeling guilty about this. If we do not allow ourselves to do this - or if we do it but then feel bad about it - then we will necessarily bring our exhaustion and negativity into many more of our interactions, undermining the good we have done the rest of the time, and curtailing our ability to do more good going forwards. Clearly, this would be counter-productive.

It would be ideal also to plan to manage things so that we can each have time away from home or at least away from family duties, doing totally different things to give us some variety and remind ourselves that there is a different dimension to life. I would say this is equally important, but we have not been great at doing this - apart from very occasional trips individually to Heartfulness meditation seminars. There doesn't seem to be the energy for it, although we know from experience that when it does happen, such things actually replenish our energy reserves. My own biggest step in this direction has been to write this book, though it has taken more than 5 years since the onset of Daniel's autism to be able to conceive that this was even possible.

These are 5 key principles that I feel are particularly important in being able to maintain a nourishing environment around our son, though I have discussed many more through the course of this book. I hope it has shown that all is not as it seems with autistic children and that there is a true wealth within them that is just waiting to be discovered and valued.   When it is, there are tremendous possibilities for these children that were never suspected before.   If a single child's life is transformed because their parents realise this through what I have written, then this book will have been worth every moment of its writing.

Resources

Transforming Autism (My Blog):
http://transformingautism.co.uk/

Mifne Centre, Israel (site includes valuable advice on identifying the early signs of autism):
http://mifne-autism.com/

National Autistic Society - http://www.autism.org.uk/

Osteopathic Centre for Children: http://occ.uk.com/

The Son Rise Programme:
http://www.autismtreatmentcenter.org/

Health and Wellness Centre: http://www.nhwc.co.uk/

Davis Method: http://www.davisautism.com/

NOIT Research: http://www.noitresearch.org/

Nordoff Robbins (Music Therapy):
-http://www.nordoff-robbins.org.uk/

Richmond Music Trust:
http://www.richmondmusictrust.org.uk/

Cerebra (Charity):   http://w3.cerebra.org.uk/

Caudwell Children's Charity:
http://www.caudwellchildren.com/

Heartfulness Meditation: http://en.heartfulness.org/

- - By The Same Author - -

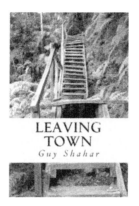

LEAVING
TOWN
Guy Shahar

Leaving Town & Other Stories

If you could make your every wish come true, would it dramatically improve the quality of your life? Gareth Field thought it would, and in 'The Goblet' he discovers the reality. You will also read about the town that nobody seems able to leave, a journey that doesn't seem to go anywhere, the potentially devastating paradoxes of travel through time, and even what happens when the lives of two young squirrels in the forest take different courses. Leaving Town is a collection of original, compelling and thought-provoking stories from the author Guy Shahar.

Available from Amazon in most countries

Printed by Amazon Italia Logistica S.r.l.
Torrazza Piemonte (TO), Italy

13376512R00130